Talk to Me God Devotionals

Volume 2

100 Modern Stories to Brighten Each Day, Deposit Wisdom, and Inspire Success

Talk to Me God Devotionals

Volume 2

100 Modern Stories to Brighten Each Day, Deposit Wisdom, and Inspire Success

Dr. Timothy Jackson Jr.

Ordering Information:

Both volumes of Talk to Me God Devotionals can be ordered directly from the author at www.talktomeGod.org. All orders from the author will be signed. Orders also by U.S. trade bookstores and wholesalers. Quantity sales. Special discounts are available on quantity purchases by corporations, associations, and others. For details, contact the publisher at the following email address: TalktoMeGodDevotionals@gmail.com

Connect with Dr. Timothy Jackson:

Instagram: www.instagram.com/iamtimjackson/
Facebook (Personal): www.facebook.com/PastorTimothy JacksonJr/
Facebook (Devotional Ministry): www.facebook.com/TalktoMe GodDevotionals/
TalktoMeGodDevotionals@gmail.com
(901) 779-6968

Dr. Timothy Jackson, Jr.
3750 Hacks Cross Road
Ste. 102-363
Memphis, TN 38125

ISBN: 979-8-218-31020-2

Dedication

This book is dedicated to my wonderful wife, Dr. Ashiqua Jackson, who has been nothing short of supportive since the very beginning. Thank you for not allowing fear and insecurity to cause me not to bring this to fruition. What a blessing you have been and continue to be.

This book is also dedicated to my wonderful children, Ava, Timothy III, and Avery. The formation of this book series began before any of you were born, but the book's finale is because of you. Not only have my experiences with you given me great stories for more devotionals, but I pray this will encourage you to pursue the greatness that is in each of you. My hope is one day, you will be as proud to have me as your father as I am to be your father. Daddy loves you more than words can ever express!

This book is also dedicated to my parents, Timothy Jackson, Sr., and my late mother, Mae Ree Jackson, who believed in me more than I believed in myself. Over the years, there have been many days I have longed to have you here, and this book is no exception. I can only imagine how excited you would be to celebrate this moment. One thing is for certain: I have and will continue to carry you with me every step of the way. I love you and miss you more than these few words can convey.

This book is also dedicated to the amazing members of Hope Fellowship Church Memphis. You are not just a congregation, but a family, and I am blessed to serve as your pastor. Your unwavering love and support have been a source of strength and joy. I eagerly anticipate our future together. Thank you!

This book is also dedicated to pastors and preachers. I pray that the devotionals you use as sermon illustrations will be a dual blessing to you and your hearers. May God abundantly bless you and your ministry.

Last but certainly not least, this book is dedicated to the supporters of the first volume of Talk to Me Devotionals. Your overwhelming support and tremendous testimonies have been a delightful surprise. I never anticipated such a response to the book. I am deeply grateful and pray that this volume will be an even greater blessing to you than the first.

Table of Contents

Look Back at It

"For I know the plans I have for you," declares the Lord, "plans to prosper you and not to harm you, plans to give you hope and a future."

—Jeremiah 29:11 (NIV)

One morning, I noticed my wife was trying to read a document in her hand. I sat across the room as she seemed to struggle to read the document she held. When she looked at the document close to her face, she was unable to read it. However, when she held the document down and away from her face, it was then that she could read it clearly. Apparently, the document she was reading needed to be at a distance to be effectively seen.

Have you ever wondered why God allowed you to experience what you faced in your life? When you were in it, you could not understand why you were where you were. You prayed, but your prayers felt as if they bounced off the ceiling of heaven. You craved and desperately sought release from a job or toxic situation, but all your efforts seemed futile. Now that you are on the other side of it, you can clearly see why. You could not see things clearly when you were in the thick of it. However, now that you are at a distance from it, you can see God's purpose for permitting it into your life. Now that you are out of the storm, you will realize you are not the same person that went into the storm. Even if you are in a storm right now, you will look back at it and thank God you came through. The greatest glory is not in never falling, but the greatest glory is getting back up again. Looking at things up close minimizes the ability to see properly.

However, when you view it from a distance, it is then that you can see it up close.

Talk to Me God

What specific challenges or situations in your life that you thought you would never escape? How did you overcome them?

How has God used what you experienced in your life or the lives of others? For instance, have you ever noticed how your past struggles have equipped you to help others going through similar situations?

Consider where you would be if it were not for what God allowed you to experience.

Wear Your Own Shoes

¹³ *For you created my inmost being;*
   you knit me together in my mother's womb.
¹⁴ *I praise you because I am fearfully and wonderfully made;*
   your works are wonderful,
   I know that full well.
¹⁵ *My frame was not hidden from you*
   when I was made in the secret place,
   when I was woven together in the depths of the earth.
¹⁶ *Your eyes saw my unformed body;*
   all the days ordained for me were written in your book
   before one of them came to be.

                                    —*Psalm 139:13-16 (NIV)*

During the twin's formative years, one of my son Timothy's
favorite things was to wear my shoes. On one occasion, he
put my shoes on and attempted to run. He did not get very
far before falling to the ground. Time and again, he tried to
run in my shoes, only to keep falling. He became increasingly
frustrated with each fall because he could not run successfully in my shoes. Finally, I said, "Son, put on your shoes and see
how well you can run." He put on his shoes and began to run
around the house.

   Many times, you can find yourself trying to do what others do, expecting similar results, but find it unfruitful and
unsuccessful. No one that is better than being you than you.
You will always fall attempting to walk in someone else's purpose, idea, or method. Nothing but frustration accompanies
attempts to be anyone other than who God called you to be.
Brene Brown is right, "Authenticity is the daily practice of

letting go of who we think we're supposed to be and embracing who we are." The time is now for you to cease endeavoring to run in someone else's shoes and do what God has gifted you to do. My brother, my sister, YOU are enough! Be yourself. Everyone is accounted for. You will always fall, trying to walk in what does not belong to you. Do what is right for you because no one else has walked or is walking in your shoes. It is only when you run in your own shoes that you will attain what God has purposed for YOU!

Talk to Me God

In what areas of your life have you tried to follow someone else's path, and what were the results of these attempts? How can recognizing your unique qualities guide you back to your own path?

Consider the scriptural reference to being "fearfully and wonderfully made." How does embracing this truth about your unique creation by God empower you to walk in your own shoes and pursue the life He has planned for you?

The Father's Shoes

" For I know the plans I have for you," declares the Lord,
"plans to prosper you and not to harm you, plans to give
you hope and a future.

—*Jeremiah 29:11 (NIV)*

In the previous devotional, I recalled that one of Timothy's
favorite things to do was to wear my shoes in his formative
years. Well, there is more to the story. On one occasion, he
put my shoes on and attempted to run. He did not get very
far before falling to the ground. He repeatedly attempted
to run in my shoes while falling to the ground. He became
increasingly frustrated with each fall because he could not
run successfully in my shoes. Finally, I said, "Son, put on your
shoes and see how well you can run." He put on his shoes
and began to run around the house. After a while of running
around the house, the time came for us to leave home. As
we prepared to go, He handed me the same shoes he tried
to wear but kept falling in. I put them on, and we headed to
where I planned to take him.

That is the story of some of our lives. We tumble into
relationships into difficult predicaments through the labyrinth of life, perpetually sliding on the slippery slopes of
life because we spend too much time trying to wear the Father's shoes. We erroneously think we can have a successful
God-pleasing life trying to wear God's shoes and do what
only God can do. We need to realize our position as children
and submit ourselves to the power of God because if we allow
Him to wear His shoes, He will take us where He would have
us go. Maybe there is an area of your life that you have not

submitted to God's control. It is time to give the Father His shoes back so God can get you where He wants to take you. As stated by Bishop Noel Jones, "God is sovereign, and when we truly understand that, we can let go of our need to control every aspect of our lives. Let God be God; you will find peace in His perfect plan."

Talk to Me God

Can you recognize moments when you have tried to take control instead of trusting God's plan? How has this affected your journey and your relationship with God?

If you think about "wearing the Father's shoes," how can giving these shoes back to God change your life's direction? What actions can you take to allow God to lead you where He wants you to be?

You Have Enough

...Simon Peter's brother spoke up, "Here is a boy with five small barley loaves and two small fish, but how far will they go among so many?

—John 6:8b-9 (NIV)

[11] *Jesus then took the loaves, gave thanks, and distributed to those who were seated as much as they wanted. He did the same with the fish.* [12] *When they had all had enough to eat, he said to his disciples, "Gather the pieces that are left over. Let nothing be wasted."*

—John 6:11-12 (NIV)

Snow is a fairly unusual occurrence in Memphis, so many people get excited when it does. School staff and children are often among those who get excited because both schools and businesses often close when snow is in the forecast. On one occasion, it snowed, and though there was little accumulation, my children were excited about the little snow there was. I stood at the window watching my children desperately search for accumulated snow to make snowballs and even build a snowman. My oldest daughter Ava was so determined that she was scooping snow that accumulated atop the barbecue grill in the backyard. The twins were getting a little snow from the ground. From the inside looking out, I concluded they would not have enough snow to build much of anything. To my surprise, they were able to build a decent-sized snowman and a sizeable snowball. Seeing the snowman and snowball, I realized just how much can be done when little is put together.

In many instances in life, you can feel as if you do not have much to work with to accomplish a certain goal. When you consider the little you have, the goal can often seem too lofty to attain. However, maybe you are not looking hard enough. You may not have much, but you assuredly have more than you think. When passion, perseverance, and purpose push you to use the little you have, you will find that God will use the little and build something with it. God will do great things for people who are willing to be faithful in the small things. My kids proved me wrong, and I want to encourage you to prove YOU wrong. All it takes is a little, and what you have is enough. Bishop TD Jakes is absolutely right: "God will use what you have to create what He has promised. Don't underestimate the little you have; it's more than enough in His hands."

Talk to Me God

How can you apply the lesson on using 'the little you have' in today's situation? Can you identify a situation where you might have undervalued your resources or abilities?

What will you do to cultivate a mindset of abundance with the resources you have, trusting in God's ability to use them to achieve His purposes in your life?

When the Script is Flipped

And we know that in all things God works for the good of those who love him, who have been called according to his purpose.

—Romans 8:28 (NIV)

When my daughter Avery was younger, she loved to write. She loved to write to the point that I kept a writing pad in my car for her. During a drive to a destination I cannot recall, she was practicing her writing in the backseat of the car. At one point, she said, "Look, Daddy, I wrote an L." I looked in the rearview mirror and said, "Avery, you wrote a great L, but in my view, it looks like a 7." My baffled toddler responded, "Daddy, how do you see a 7 when I wrote an L?" She did not comprehend how her L became a 7. She was doing it correctly, but her father's view in the mirror saw a 7 and not an L.

If you've spent more than five minutes in a church, you'll likely notice that Christians hold the number seven in high regard because it symbolizes completeness. The Christian life is filled with many ups, downs, highs, lows, mountains, and valleys. Sometimes we win, and sometimes we lose. When we lose, we often refer to the loss as an *L*. However, God has an amazing way of flipping our Ls into completions. In every loss, God divinely weaves our Ls for our good. No matter what losses you have experienced or are experiencing, you cannot afford to get trapped in the L. I agree with Joel Osteen, "God has a way of bringing out the best in us through the most difficult circumstances." You must keep moving forward because one day, you will look in the rearview mirror of your life and conclude that God completed every L you

9

experienced. There is no L that God cannot flip, and when He flips it, completion happens at the same time.

Talk to Me God

Think back to a time in your life when you encountered what seemed like a loss or failure, only to later realize it was part of God's plan for your growth. How did this shift in perspective impact your faith?

What challenges are you currently facing (Ls) that you might find difficult to see as part of God's plan? How can you develop a mindset that trusts God to turn these challenges into opportunities for growth?

The Flintstones of Life

A friend loves at all times, and a brother is born for adversity.

—*Proverbs 17:17 (NIV)*

As iron sharpens iron, so one person sharpens another.

—*Proverbs 27:17(NIV)*

Growing up, the Flintstones was one of my favorite cartoons. The main characters were Fred, Barney, Betty, and Wilma, all of which were best friends. What I admired most about the friendship of Fred/Barney and Wilma/Betty is they never withheld the truth from one another. In each moment Fred was about to do something wrong or something that would not be in his best interest, Barney would chime in, "I don't know Fred, that's not good because..." In short, Barney held Fred accountable, always desiring Fred to always do the right thing. Oftentimes, Fred would get upset and yell at Barney because he did not respond well to accountability. However, despite Barney's awareness of Fred's disdain for the truth, he did not waver in proclaiming the truth. Barney was fervent in his attempt to be a true friend to Fred. The same dynamic could also be witnessed in the friendship of Wilma and Betty.

In life, everyone needs a Flintstone. The Flintstones of your life are those people who do not tell us what we want to hear and do not tell us what we should hear. They are people who give us advice that is in line with the will of God and in our best interest. Everyone needs that someone who will say, "I don't know (insert your name), that's not good to do because..." The reality is that true friends always want to see

11

their friends walk and live in truth, even if telling the truth will trigger a tantrum. It has been said that the most valuable gift we can receive is an honest friend, and a true friend will hold us accountable for being our best selves. Oscar Wilde says it this way, "a true friend stabs you from the front." We all need at least one Barney/Betty in our lives. Conversely, let us strive to be a Barney/Betty in someone else's life.

Talk to Me God

Who are you withholding the truth from? Pray and commit to sharing the truth with them in love.

Who are the Barneys/Bettys in your life? Write down how their sharing of truth was a blessing to you.

Still Tipping

Bear with each other and forgive one another if any of you has a grievance against someone. Forgive as the Lord forgave you.

—*Colossians 3:13 (NIV)*

[8] *For it is by grace you have been saved, through faith–and this not from yourselves, it is the gift of God* [9] *not by works, so that no one can boast.*

—*Ephesians 2:8-9 (NIV)*

Have you ever eaten at a restaurant with friends and received bad service? It took what seemed to be hours to get your food. When the food arrived at the table, it was cold, and the server had the audacity to have an attitude when you said something about it! It seemed that your glass was always empty because they never came back to refill it! You asked for the check, and they didn't split it up (like you told them to)! At the end of the meal, the server still has an attitude. You have paid, and now comes the decision of whether you will leave a tip. What do you do?

How many times have we given God bad service? How often have we neglected to do what He specifically told us to do? How many times have we done what God told us not to do, and we did the opposite anyway? All of us have given God bad *service* to some degree. The truth is that no matter how bad our service to God is or has been, God continues to *tip* us on a perpetual basis. God *tips* us by allowing us to wake up each morning. God *tips* us with the provision of health and strength. God *tips* us by keeping clothes on our backs. The list goes on about the many 'tips' God blesses us with despite our unscrupulous service to Him. Those of us who are recipients of grace should be distributors of grace. The next time you have a terrible experience in a restaurant or another venue requiring a tip, consider the continuous grace extended to you. As a matter of fact, even at this very moment, God is still tipping. Thank God for grace!

Talk to Me God

Apply to Your Own Life: How has God shown you grace despite times when your 'service' to Him may not have been perfect? How can recognizing those moments of grace influence your actions toward others?

The next time you have a rough situation—like lousy service at a restaurant—how can you apply the principle of grace? What practical ways can you extend grace, mirroring the forgiveness and patience God extends to you?

Bifocal Vision

"I am the Lord, the God of all mankind. Is anything too hard for me?"

—*Jeremiah 32:27 (NIV)*

The purpose of bifocals is to give an individual the ability to see things two different ways at the same time. The lenses are divided into two different parts. One part of the lens is for seeing things closely, and the other is for seeing things from far away. The prescription determines whether the majority of the lens is designed for nearsightedness (to improve close-up vision) or farsightedness (to enhance distance vision). The benefit of bifocals is that you can always see no matter what you are looking at, no matter how close, no matter how far, no matter how small, no matter how big, no matter where it is.

In life, we need spiritual bifocals when it comes to the giants we face. With spiritual bifocals, no matter what a situation is, no matter how small, no matter how big, no matter its locale, we can still see God. There are times in your life when things are simply too big for you to handle, but you need to know that God is bigger than whatever you face. With bifocal vision, you should come to the conclusion that God is greater than your past, your pain, your shame, the fear, the anxiety, occupational challenges, divorce, bankruptcy, and any other vicissitudes of life. When life lands you in difficult spaces, the enemy desires that you remain nearsighted, only seeing what is before you. Of course, it is impossible *not* to see what you are in, but God desires that you be God-sighted, to see past what you are in and see God. As one quote says, "Your present circumstances don't determine where you can go; they merely determine where you start." Whatever or whoever is before you is never bigger than the God that is for you. God longs to be the One you trust to get you through, the One to deliver you, the One to strengthen you, and the One to keep you through the storm.

Talk to Me God

Think about your current challenges. Have you been near-sighted or God-sighted? Explain.

Considering the metaphor of bifocals, how can you actively cultivate a vision that addresses immediate issues and keeps God's larger plan in view? What practical steps can you take to maintain this dual focus in your daily life?

The Life of Popeye

When my soul fainted within me, I remembered the LORD;
And my prayer went up to You, Into Your holy temple.

—Jonah 2:7 (NKJV)

Behold, I give you the authority to trample on serpents
and scorpions, and over all the power of the enemy, and
nothing shall by any means hurt you.

—Luke 10:19 (NIV)

Popeye was another childhood cartoon favorite. In this cartoon, Popeye frequently fights with a burly man named Bluto. The source of contention between Popeye and Bluto was Bluto's persistent pursuit of Popeye's wife, Olive Oil. In each episode, Bluto tirelessly attempted to sway Olive Oil's attention toward him. Oftentimes, it would seem as if Bluto was getting the best of Popeye, and he would ultimately lose what seemed to be a never-ending battle. However, when the battle became too much, Popeye realized he needed some additional strength. To increase his strength, he would quickly consume a can of spinach. Amazingly, every time the spinach was consumed, Popeye would immediately be strengthened and easily defeat Bluto because the spinach gave him extraordinary strength to overcome his enemy.

As the people of God, we have a daily fight with an enemy who tirelessly attempts to destroy our lives. As with Bluto, Satan is persistent in his attempts, and he takes advantage of every opportunity he has to try to sway our attention from what and who we hold dear. If we are honest, there are moments when it seems as if Satan is getting the best of us. In fact, at some points, we feel like we are losing this never-ending battle, and we need some additional strength. It is in these moments that we need to stop trying to handle things in our own might and consume the spinach of Scripture and prayer to tap into the extraordinary strength we need to overcome. We do not fight *for* victory; we fight *from* victory, but we cannot win without the weaponry of the Word of God.

Talk to Me God

What are you trying to handle in your own strength?

Meditate on the above Scriptures and list some that are relevant to your life.

Pray and ask God to provide you with extraordinary strength to handle what is before you.

It Stinks—Part I

... let us throw off everything that hinders and the sin that so easily entangles. And let us run with perseverance the race marked out for us, ² fixing our eyes on Jesus, the pioneer and perfecter of faith.

—Hebrews 12:1b-2a (NIV)

For years, my children begged my wife and I for a dog. We refused to succumb to their request for multiple reasons, so we compromised by buying fish for the three of them (don't judge us! ☺). Over time, each fish began to die one by one. My son's fish was the last to die. When his fish died, he had an interesting response: he refused to get rid of his dead fish. Attempting to be sensitive to his young heart, we allowed the dead fish to remain on his bathroom counter. As one can imagine, it was not long before the dead fish began to stink up the entire bathroom. Unfortunately, the odor wasn't confined to just the bathroom; it permeated a significant portion of our home simply because of a refusal to part with that which was dead.

If we are not careful, we will allow people dead things and even dead people to stay in our lives. Many times, we allow love, convenience, and longevity to cause us to allow them to remain in our lives. The truth of the matter is when there is a refusal to release dead things/people in your life; they will stink up various areas of your life. These areas include but are not limited to your health, finances, credit, and even other people you are connected to. In truth, the longer you allow them to stay in your life, the more they will stink up your life. Though it may be difficult to let them go, it is necessary. Mandy Hale is right, "Toxic people will pollute everything around them. Don't hesitate. Fumigate."

Talk to Me God

Can you think of any 'dead things' in your life: habits, relationships, past grievances, whatever, that you have held onto for longer than you should have? How has this impacted your well-being, and how else has it influenced your life?

What kinds of steps do you take to start this process of discarding these things that are toxic from your life? How might getting rid of these burdens improve your spiritual and emotional health?

It Stinks—Part II

... Let us throw off everything that hinders and the sin that so easily entangles. And let us run with perseverance the race marked out for us, ² fixing our eyes on Jesus, the pioneer and perfecter of faith.

— *Hebrews 12:1b-2a (NIV)*

Yesterday's devotional talked about the death of my son's fish and its impact on our home. One evening, I made a sneaky attempt to give it a private burial in the porcelain cemetery in his bathroom. It goes without saying that I was excited to finally be forever relieved of the foul odor that permeated our home. Unfortunately, just as I was about to flush it, my son walked in. When he took notice of my attempt, his face flooded with tears, crying profusely, begging me not to do it. I wish I could tell you that I ignored his cry, but I cannot. I simply placed the stinky container containing the dead fish back on the counter, and the foul odor continued. I was so weak to my son's plea that I allowed the fish to remain for longer than I'd like to admit. We had literally become accustomed to living with the dead to the point we were anesthetized to its impact on our home. The dead fish remained for weeks to the point that after a while, we did not smell it anymore.

Hopefully, yesterday, you decided to let go of who and what is stinking up your life. While that can be incredibly difficult, today, I want you to take inventory of the loss(es). Are there areas of your life that have been negatively impacted by their activity and presence? What would your life look like if you let them go? Maybe it's been a while since you have given this some thought. Maybe you have not thought about it at all. Have you become so accustomed to losing that you no longer know how to win? My friend, sometimes you need to release what is causing you harm, even though letting go may be painful. Otherwise, you run the risk of becoming accustomed to living with the dead habits and people to the degree you are anesthetized to their impact.

Talk to Me God

Have you ever had the experience of being so used to something negative, either a situation or a relationship, that the harm from that adverse condition no longer affects you as it used to? What made you realize this was a need for change?

How do the advantages of finally letting go of what has kept you back or caused detriment in life stack up? How can you start with this process and guarantee a healthier environment for yourself and others?

Your Father Is Bigger than Where You Are

Yours, Lord, is the greatness and the power and the glory and the majesty and the splendor, for everything in heaven and earth is yours. Yours, Lord, is the kingdom; you are exalted as head over all.

—I Chronicles 29:11 (NIV)

On a hot, muggy May afternoon in the city, I went to a field day at my kid's school. Between games, my daughter Avery and her class sat under a canopy while my son and his class were seated under a tent that someone brought. Having twins, I vacillated between both areas to ensure I supported them equally. When I walked up to the tent where my son Timothy was, I was taller than the tent, so I stayed just outside. Immediately noticing my height in contrast to the tent, he walked over to me and loudly proclaimed to his classmates and everyone in the area, "My daddy is tall. My daddy is taller than the tent!" Though I was uncomfortable with the sudden attention, it was clear that my son wanted to bring attention to the fact that his father was bigger than the place he was in.

Where are you today? I am not speaking of your physical location, but where are you mentally, emotionally, academically, socially, financially, and spiritually? Prayerfully, you are in a place of contentment and security. However, frustration, discontentment, unhappiness, misery, anger, or distress may be more appropriate descriptors of where you are. Wherever you are, know that your Father God is bigger than the place you are in. God is greater than your pain. God is greater than your failures. God is greater than your fears. God is bigger than whatever you are in and wherever you are. When you focus on your problems, you'll have more problems. When you focus on God, you will ultimately have more peace.

Talk to Me God

Reflect on your emotional, mental, spiritual, and financial conditions. In what areas of your life do you feel pressed and limited? How might the realization of the greatness of God bring a new perspective to these situations?

How can concentrating on God's presence and power in your life lead you to experience more peace despite the challenges or "tents" you might find yourself under? What actionable steps can you take to shift your focus from your problems to His provision?

Put It All in His Hands

Casting all your care upon Him, for He cares for you.

—I Peter 5:7 (NKJV)

And this same God who takes care of me will supply all your needs from his glorious riches, which have been given to us in Christ Jesus.

—Philippians 4:19 (NLT)

On the first day of school, my youngest daughter, Avery, was given a list of supplies she needed for her classroom. I was in our bedroom as she and her brother came home. After arriving home, she immediately went into the bedroom, kissed me, and handed me the list of things she needed. Interestingly, as she handed it to me, she did not say anything about the list or even tell me where it came from. She simply handed it to me and walked away as if to say, "I have done my part." I watched her walk away with an obvious assurance that she knew her daddy was going to take care of everything on her list. Her sole role was to place what she needed in my hands.

We all have needs—physical needs, emotional needs, spiritual needs, financial needs, and the list goes on. Many times, we look around at ourselves and at others around us in an effort to get our needs met. This is often without even the thought of placing our needs in the Father's Hands. When we put it in His Hands, we can walk in assurance, knowing that God will handle everything we need when we give it to Him. There is an old song that says, "All in His Hands, I put it all in His Hands. This and that, I put it all in His Hands. He can handle it; that's a fact. I put it all in His Hands." Worrying does not erase the problems of tomorrow, but worrying certainly erases the peace you can enjoy today. Whatever needs exist in your life today, put it all in His Hands.

Talk to Me God

What are your current needs or concerns that you find it hard to entrust to God? How does the simple act of Avery turning over her list to her father inspire you to do the same with your burdens?

How will adopting a mindset of trusting God with all your needs affect your daily peace and overall well-being? What steps are you going to take to start really letting go of your worries and really placing them in his hands? Imagine the sense of freedom and light-heartedness that comes from releasing these burdens.

Have Some Fun

¹ There is a time for everything, and a season for every activity under heaven: ⁴ a time to weep and a time to laugh, a time to mourn and a time to dance.

—Ecclesiastes 3:1, 4 (NIV)

During my early years of ministry, I served as a Youth Pastor at my home church. On one trip, the youth got together and strategically planned how they would set me up and give me an ice shower. They even convinced the Youth Director and other adults to assist them in their plot. After being warned about their plan, I was able to avoid the ice shower for a while. However, they remained steadfast in their plan and finally got me! I figured they would not think I would retaliate, but I constructed a plan of my own and blessed them with ice showers of their own. The next few nights were filled with laughter and fun, and the youth had an opportunity to experience their Youth Pastor, Youth Director, and other adults in another way outside of ministering to them.

When people think of Christianity, one word that rarely comes to mind is *fun*. Stiff, strict, and boring are more probable descriptions. So often in our journey with God, we forget to relax and have some fun. Many people are turned off because of their encounters with overly serious Christians. These are those people who preach in everything they say. They never laugh, never play, never have a good time, never go anyplace outside of church, and the list goes on. Here is the reality - God never meant for His people to be boring. We see many moments of relaxation and fun throughout the Scriptures. The music was so loud in Luke 15 that the older son heard music and dancing in the distance! That must have been some kind of party! As believers, being godly and having a good time can coexist. There is a blessing in rest, relaxation, and recreation. Have some fun, and honor God in your fun!

Talk to Me God

When was the last time you had fun outside of something church/ministry-related?

Plan something fun to do this week. Ex. massage, go to the movies, nice dinner, etc.

It's How You Look at It

Finally, brothers and sisters, whatever is true, whatever is noble, whatever is right, whatever is pure, whatever is lovely, whatever is admirable—if anything is excellent or praiseworthy—think about such things.

—Philippians 4:8 (NIV)

While using an electric shaver, I noticed the display showed 66%. I immediately thought to myself that it would not be long before I needed to charge it. However, upon closer inspection, I realized that I was looking at the display upside down. I saw 66% but in reality it was 99%. Clearly it was not as low as I thought, I was simply not looking at it properly.

When we find ourselves in challenging situations and circumstances, we can be tempted to think of the glass as half empty. Negative thoughts and worse-case scenarios fill our minds to overflowing. If we are not careful, we will even begin to prepare for the worse to happen. Obviously, this devotional is not an attempt to diminish what life may be throwing your way. However, it is an attempt to shift you to look at things differently. Oftentimes, we are simply looking at life upside down. You have seen better days, but *everything* is not all bad. When it comes to the things in our lives, we look at things incorrectly and arrive at inaccurate conclusions. When you view your life from the proper vantage point, you may realize you didn't lose as much as you thought. You have much more left in your than you thought you had. My friend, all is not lost. Perspective is everything. The way you see a problem will either be your problem or your progress. You may not have everything you desire, but you certainly have all you need. Just because areas of your life may be upside down, all of life is not. Perspective is the key difference between a mountain and a molehill. It's all in how you look at it.

Talk to Me God

List what you desire to be different in your life.

List what is positive in your life.

Take a moment to focus and meditate on everything that is positive and pray about what you desire to be different.

Go Through Customs

¹³ *Brethren, I count not myself to have apprehended: but this one thing I do, forgetting those things which are behind, and reaching forth unto those things which are before,* ¹⁴ *I press toward the mark for the prize of the high calling of God in Christ Jesus.*

—Proverbs 3:13-14 (KJV)

A few years ago, some friends and I traveled to an area outside of the United States. After touring and shopping in the area, we were ready to return to the states. However, for us to get return to the states, we needed to cross the border. In order to cross the border, we had to first go through a security screening. The purpose of the security screening was to ensure that illegal items were not being transported into the country. As we passed through security, it was fascinating to see tables stacked with assortment of items people attempted to bring into country. The items were considered illegal in the U.S., but legal in the other area, therefore the items had to be left at customs.

Along the journey of life, all of us were once outside God's borders. All of us were unsaved at one point in time. All of us have done some things we are not proud of. We have been some places we are not proud of. Nevertheless, there came a point when we decided to cross the border into God's family. As we establish a deeper relationship with God, there is a screening process we must go through. Many of us have difficulty with this because there are people, things, and habits we wish to accompany us into the relationship. Unfortunately, certain people things, and habits that were

31

acceptable in one dimension may be deemed illegal in the next dimension. Everyone around you may not understand your journey, but ultimately that is your responsibility. When you assess your circle and your life, you may make some discoveries of who and what may need to be left behind as you journey toward the destiny God has for you.

Talk to Me God

Make a list of your closest relatives/friends.

Do they impact your life positively/negatively.

It Has to Die

...let us strip off every weight that slows us down, especially the sin that so easily trips us up. And let us run with endurance the race God has set before us. ^{2} We do this by keeping our eyes on Jesus, the champion who initiates and perfects our faith. Because of the joy awaiting him, he endured the cross, disregarding its shame. Now, he is seated in the place of honor beside God's throne. ^{3} Think of all the hostility he endured from sinful people; then you won't become weary and give up.

—Hebrews 12:1-3 (NLT)

A fly had gotten into my house, ultimately disturbing my sleep all night because somehow it had gotten into my bedroom. As I prepared for bed the next night, I heard the fly buzzing around in the bathroom. Hearing it flying around irritated me to the core. I immediately determined that the fly was going to die that night, no matter how long it took me to kill it. I was resolute that the previous night was the last night I would allow the fly to disturb me. I closed off everything in the bathroom in order to isolate the irritant. I needed to kill that which was guilty of disturbing me. My mind was made up that the fly had to die, and it had to die that night. I had had enough!

This may be your story. You have had some things (possibly even some people) buzzing around your life, disturbing your house, marriage, work, dreams, etc. Your irritant may not be included in this brief list, but you know exactly what is disturbing you. Today, make the determination that you have had enough. Do what you need to do to get where you need to be. Disregard the longevity, the presumed loyalty, and the family dynamic, and *kill it* to restore your peace. Make up your mind that it must die, and it must die right now. Haven't you had enough?

Talk to Me God

What is a continual disturbance to your peace?

Why do you allow the disturbance(s) to remain?

Take the first step toward regaining your peace today.

Pop Quiz

² But his delight is in the law of the LORD, and on his law, he meditates day and night. ³ He is like a tree planted by streams of water, which yields its fruit in season and whose leaf does not wither. Whatever he does prospers.

—*Psalm 1:2-3 (NIV)*

Pop quizzes are fairly common for high school or college students. A pop quiz is a mini-test to determine if one is retaining the information they have learned up to that point. Because of the ever-present possibility of a pop quiz, a student needs to be perpetually prepared just in case. When I was in college, it was important that I continually pondered what I learned in class so I could be confident I would pass a pop quiz with flying colors.

Have you ever noticed that something happens that threatens to throw you off course when things seem to be going well? "It is always something" has become your regular mantra. When you get some extra money, something breaks or needs repair. When you strengthen your relationship with God, some person, place, or thing challenges you to regress. Immediately following an awesome worship experience, at a church, someone upsets you in the parking lot or grocery store. When one class is going great, another goes downhill. You get the picture...pop quizzes! The enemy wants to see if we are not only retaining but also living out those things we learn can claim to believe in the Word of God. As children of God, it is imperative that we continually meditate on God's Word, so we will always be prepared and able to pass the enemy's pop quiz(zes) with flying colors! Whatever you may be going through now, it's just a pop quiz—and its open book!

Talk to Me God

When challenges arise, what is one thing you can commit to doing to strengthen your faith and resilience?

How can you encourage others who may be experiencing challenges?

Sit In It

But many who are first will be last, and the last first.

—Mark 10:31 (NIV)

I had the blessed privilege of going to the Holy Land and visiting some incredible sites. While at the Mount of Precipice, our group assembled on the benches to hear a guide speak. When I came up, the only place that was available for me to sit was a space in the back with dried poop on the bench. I hesitantly sat down in that place while silently resenting the fact that I was in the back. Interestingly, after the guide had been speaking for a while, our group leader, who was behind me, told everyone to turn around. Suddenly, I was now in the front— despite having sat in poop and feeling unhappy about being at the back (or so I thought). I realized that it was my willingness to endure the discomfort and temporary unpleasantness that brought me to the front.

There are times in life when it seems that you feel you are not where you thought you would be at certain points in your life. Surely by now the degree would have been obtained, the home would have been purchased, a wedding band would be on the left hand, and children would be in the backseat of the car, among many other things. However, that is not where life has landed you. In fact, there are times when you feel as if you are sitting in the mess of life. Not only are you not where you thought you would be at this point, but you are experiencing things you never thought or desired to experience. You never thought your life would be this messy. You need to know that despite the place you are in, remain where you are because God is standing behind you and will soon turn your situation around. Hang in there; God is going to bless you even in your mess.

Talk to Me God

What things did you think would have happened to/for you by now?

How do you feel about it? Angry? Disappointed? Frustrated?

Pray and ask God for patience and encouragement.

Focus on Your Own Lane

Therefore, since we are surrounded by such a great cloud of witnesses, let us throw off everything that hinders and the sin that so easily entangles. And let us run with perseverance the race marked out for us

—Hebrews 12:1 (NIV)

For I know the plans I have for YOU," declares the Lord, "plans to prosper YOU and not to harm YOU, plans to give YOU hope and a future.

—Jeremiah 29:11 (NIV)

During swim lessons with my children, the instructors allowed two young ladies to engage in a race to the other side of the pool. When the instructor gave the signal, the girls began swimming to the end of the pool while all the parents were perched on the bank, anxiously anticipating who would win. Because one of the young ladies was clearly a stronger swimmer, we thought the race was over before it began. However, to our surprise, she lost. As she exited the pool, she hung her head in disappointment, wiped her face, and said, "I lost because I kept looking over at her."

This is the story of many of our lives; we are losing because we are focused on what is happening in the lives of those around us. Because we are so engaged in their story, we have paused the penning of our own story. It has been said, "Every moment you spend wishing you had someone else's life is a moment you spend wasting yours." If we ever desire to win, we must focus solely on our life's lane. Peering other people's lanes will always result in disappointment and us forfeiting things and opportunities that should be ours. Iyan-la Vanzant once said, "Comparing yourself to others in an act of violence against your authentic self." Like the moon and the sun have their moments to shine, your moment is also coming. In the meantime, focus on your own lane because your focus will determine your reality.

Talk to Me God

Whose life/lives do you admire?

What are the specific things you admire about their lives?

Consider the things in your life that others potentially admire. Pray and ask God for a spirit of contentment and possibly for-giveness for taking your own blessings for granted.

They Will Dry Up

¹ The Lord is my light and my salvation—
whom shall I fear?
The Lord is the stronghold of my life—
of whom shall I be afraid?
² When the wicked advance against me
to devour me,
it is my enemies and my foes
who will stumble and fall.
³ Though an army besiege me,
my heart will not fear;
though war break out against me,
even then I will be confident.

—Psalm 27:1-3 (NIV)

While walking with kids at a local park, I noticed dried-up worms along the way. The day of sunshine was welcomed after the previous day was filled with rainstorms. Though worms made their way out, it became abundantly clear that worms were unable to survive in the unrelenting sun. Though worms thrive well in wet and shady conditions, they dry up and die in the sun. Their biological makeup does not permit them the ability to withstand too much sun. As we encountered the dried worms along the way, we simply stepped over them and continued toward our destination.

Many times, we are surrounded by worms. Worms? Yes, worms! Worms are people who are full of drama and have an insatiable appetite for commotion and discord. Unfortunately, they seem to thrive in shady conditions. When faced with these kinds of people, it is tempting to think there is a need to *kill* them by firing them, removing them from the position, sending an e-mail, or whatever weaponry one may prefer. However, that is not always necessary (though sometimes it is). The main thing to remember is that if and when you stay in the SON, the worms will dry up without assistance. Mandy Hale once said, "Don't waste words on people who deserve your silence. Sometimes, the most powerful thing you can say is nothing at all." Soon, you will be stepping over them as you journey to your destination.

Talk to Me God

Have you met "worms"—people doing really well at creating chaos and making a drama out of every little thing? How has this impacted your life, and how do you navigate it?

How does staying on your spiritual path and trusting the guidance of God help you deal with difficult people or situations without getting mixed up with unnecessary conflict? What are some of the things you could do to embody this more consistently?

In the Waiting Room

Wait for the LORD; be strong and take heart and wait for the LORD.

—Psalm 27:14 (NIV)

But they that wait upon the Lord shall renew their strength; they shall mount up with wings as eagles; they shall run, and not be weary; and they shall walk, and not faint.

—Isaiah 40:31 (NIV)

Several years ago, a sick family member spent several days in the hospital. The family spent most of the days and nights in the waiting room each day. While in the waiting room, the family would pray together and anxiously wait for doctors to come and provide us with an update on the health of our loved one. In the waiting room, we were unaware of our loved one's condition; we prayed continuously while we waited. We just trusted that the doctor(s) would usher us out of the waiting room when the time was right. Admittedly, it was difficult not knowing anything, but it was the hospital's policy for us to remain in the waiting room.

Have you ever found yourself in a situation where you were completely unsure of what to do or which direction to take? When you had no idea what might happen next? When you were praying and seeking guidance from God, only to feel like He was silent? My friend, you are in the waiting room. While in the waiting room, you must trust that God has everything under control and will bring you out in His time, not yours. Yes, it is difficult not knowing the specifics of the future, but it is beyond your control and rests in God's hands. While you may feel waiting is wasting, know that God is working while you wait. My friend, complete faith in God also comprises complete faith in God's timing. Dr. Jeremiah Wright declares, "Waiting on God is not passive; it's an active trust in His promises and His plan for your life." In this season, your role is to remain prayerful and KNOW that God is going to bring you out. Meanwhile, there are pages in the divine policy of our lives when we are called to remain in the waiting room.

Talk to Me God

Think about when you were waiting for something meaningful and didn't know what would happen. How did you keep believing things would work out?

What can you do to stay patient and trust in God's plan when you're in a waiting period? How can you make this waiting time meaningful?

Just Taste It

⁷ The angel of the LORD encamps around those who fear him, and he delivers them.

⁸ Taste and see that the LORD is good; blessed is the man who takes refuge in him.

⁹ Fear the LORD, you his saints, for those who fear him lack nothing.

—Psalm 34:7-9 (NIV)

As a child, there were certain foods I simply did not like to eat. There were many reasons why I refused to eat certain things. Look, texture, smell, or simply knowing what it was (i.e., pig feet) were a few of my reasons (or should I say excuses?). When faced with a decision to eat the food in front of me, my mother would say, "Just taste it. You don't know if you will like it unless you taste it and it's good for you." Needless to say, I tasted some foods I didn't like initially, and they turned out to be some of my favorite things to eat.

For many of us, there are certain things and areas we just do not wish to taste. Because what is before us is unfamiliar, we draw the conclusion that we do not want to partake. The uncertainty associated with the change causes discomfort. Therefore, we take the easier route and conveniently decline. This list can go on and on about the areas God wants to lead some of us to, but we refuse to taste it. Are you refusing to taste an opportunity God has placed before you? God is saying to us, "Just taste it; you don't know if you will like it unless you taste it, and it's good for you—and those connected to you." One thing is for certain: you will never know what you are capable of until you try it. To wrap it up, Thomas Jefferson stated, "If you want something you've never had, you must be willing to do something you've never done."

Talk to Me God

Think about a time when you were hesitant to try something new because it was unfamiliar or uncomfortable. What happened when you finally tried it?

Are there opportunities or changes that God might be encouraging you to try right now? How can you overcome your hesitation to discover if they are beneficial for you?

Be Thankful for the Adjustment

"7 You used to walk in these ways, in the life you once lived. 8 But now you must rid yourselves of all such things as these: anger, rage, malice, slander, and filthy language from your lips. 9 Do not lie to each other, since you have taken off your old self with its practices 10 and have put on the new self, which is being renewed in knowledge in the image of its Creator."

—Colossians 3:7-10 (NIV)

While at a friend's home, I noticed the plastic installation stickers that remained on a sound system she had purchased. After asking her about it, she told me the stickers had been on the radio since it was purchased two years ago! After laughing and joking about the stickers not being removed, I peeled them off and threw them away. She then said, "Now it doesn't look right!" The system did not look right because she had become accustomed to seeing the stickers on it. After a short while, she adjusted to seeing the system without the stickers because that was what it was supposed to look like anyway.

While giving your life to Christ is the absolute best thing a person can do, the truth is that it can be uncomfortable in some ways. It can be uncomfortable releasing things that you once held dear. It can be uncomfortable saying no to people and things you once readily said yes to. Those adjustments are uncomfortable because you have become accustomed to living your life a certain way. In a real sense, there are some things you peeled off that you never imagined being without.

However, after a while, you adjust to your new life in Christ and find great joy in the adjustments you made. Today, be thankful that God assisted you in making the adjustment to live a life more in conformity with His Word. The adjustment to a new way of life is how God purposed it to be anyway.

Talk to Me God

Have you ever experienced discomfort from changing an old habit or behavior? Reflect on how you adapted and the benefits it brought.

Identify some aspects of your life that could be realigned with God's teachings. How can gratitude for these necessary adjustments enhance your acceptance and commitment to them?

Unrealized Protection

²⁴ *Now to Him who is able to keep you from stumbling,*
And to present you faultless Before the presence of His
glory with exceeding joy, ²⁵ *To God our Savior, Who alone*
is wise, Be glory and majesty, Dominion and power, Both
now and forever. Amen.

—Jude 1:24-25 (NIV)

A little boy and his older brother attended a basketball game.
While they were watching the game, suddenly, the little boy
decided to run onto the court while the game was going on.
He was totally unaware he could get hurt if he got onto the
court while the game was being played. However, before he
could get to the court, his older brother grabbed him. Interestingly, the little boy was upset because he wanted to be on
the court. Nevertheless, his older brother was out to protect
him from the danger he did not see.

There are times when we unknowingly walk into dangerous or even toxic situations. Sometimes, we are totally unaware of the dangers that lurk ahead. However, the blessing
is that God grabs us before we get to the dangers. Some of
us have been rescued from accidents, robberies, bad job situations, bad relationships, rape, murder, among many other
things! Nevertheless, we sometimes get upset because things
in our lives sometimes do not go as planned. However, it is
during these times that we should bear in mind that our God
may be protecting us from the dangers we do not see. Divine
forces are continuously at work shielding those who believe
in God's protection.

Talk to Me God

Have you ever been frustrated when things didn't go your way? Can you think of a time when this might have kept you safe from harm?

How can recognizing God's protection help you stay calm and trusting when unexpected changes happen? What can you do to remember this protection in challenging times?

Rest Yourself Before You Wreck Yourself

In peace I will lie down and sleep, for you alone, Lord, make me dwell in safety. —

Psalm 4:8 (NIV)

² He makes me lie down in green pastures,
he leads me beside quiet waters,
³ he refreshes my soul.
He guides me along the right paths
for his name's sake.

—Psalm 23:2-3 (NIV)

On a beautiful Wednesday afternoon in Houston, I was walking into a restaurant with my friends when I noticed a totaled tow truck at a salvage yard next door. As we looked at the damage, we were fascinated by the fact oxymoron that it was a totaled tow truck was total. It is oxymoronic that the tow truck, which is in the business of carrying wrecked vehicles, is itself wrecked. What was accustomed to carrying the broken found itself in a position of having to be carried.

To live a life of service is the goal for believers. While God has called us to serve in various ways, living a life of service is lived out to the point that it is self-destructive. I am talking about people who devote so much of their time and energy to providing for other people that they literally have no time for themselves. What's more, some people do for other people to the extent that it has a negative impact on their own health. working long hours to meet the company's

51

goals, shuttling children everywhere, acting as a proverbial bank for friends and family—the list goes on. Can you relate? You can spend so much time caring for others that, if you're not careful, you might find yourself mentally, physically, and emotionally exhausted, and financially drained. My friend, an empty lantern cannot provide light, and self-care is the way to fuel yourself so that you can give light to other people. As with the tow truck mentioned above, you are no good to anyone else when you are broken. L.R. Knost remarked, "Taking care of yourself doesn't mean *me first*, it means *me too*." Be careful that you do not *total* yourself because you are too busy carrying other people. You owe yourself what you give so freely to others. When you take care of you, you can give the world the best of you rather than what's left of you.

Talk to Me God

Who or what is consuming a great deal of your time and energy?

Plan to take some time for yourself in the next seven days. Take out your calendar and fully commit to a day and time. It can be 30 minutes, an hour, or a day, but commit to some "me time."

He Kept Knocking

"Here I am! I stand at the door and knock. If anyone hears my voice and opens the door, I will come in and eat with him, and he with me."

—*Revelation 3:20 (NIV)*

Can you imagine going to someone's house every day, all day, knocking on the door? You knock in the morning, afternoon, evening, and throughout the night. They are trying to sleep, but you keep knocking. Night after night, week after week, and year after year, you are at the door and continue to be ignored. Many of us would leave after a few knocks, let alone continuous knocking!

Night after night, week after week, and year after year, Jesus relentlessly knocked on the doors of our hearts. Relationship after relationship, He kept knocking. Despite the habit, He kept knocking. Sin had a chokehold, but He kept knocking. No matter what we endeavored to do to ignore Him, Jesus continued to knock in hopes of one day being allowed to come in. His life is relentless, unwavering, and resolute. As children of God, we should praise Him for continuing to knock on the door of our hearts despite everything we did, said, or thought. It is vital that we pray for others that Jesus is allowed to come in from the porch of their hearts. When we think about the privilege of a relationship with Christ, we should be thankful that He kept knocking!

<u>Talk to Me God</u>

Reflect on the moment you allowed Jesus to come into your heart.

Pray for those in your family or circle of friends that they will allow Jesus into their hearts.

It's On the Other Side

*20 From the fruit of his mouth a man's stomach is filled;
with the harvest from his lips he is satisfied. 21 The tongue
has the power of life and death, and those who love it will
eat its fruit.*

—*Proverbs 18:20-21 (NIV)*

There was a Christian young man who was getting frustrated
with things taking place in his life. It seemed that it was one
thing after another. In one month, he dealt with the passing
of a loved one; things were going wrong in his home, and
things were happening to his car. Therefore, he began to
think, what next? However, when he found himself starting
to get down and discouraged, he began to speak positively
about his situation(s) to help him get through. Eventually, he
made it to the other side and was able to see what God was
trying to show him through his experiences.

Can you relate to this young man? It seems that one thing
happens after another. Even as a Christian, you can sometimes find yourself frustrated, wondering what's next. When
these moments happen, we must learn to think and speak
positively about our situations, no matter how difficult they
are. We cannot think or speak negatively and expect to get
through and see what God is trying to reveal. A negative perspective blinds you from seeing the blessing on the other side
of the trials. Whatever you may be going through, think and
speak positively about your situation and KNOW that God
has a blessing on the other side.

Talk to Me God

Recall a tough time when you felt overwhelmed by continuous challenges. How did changing your perspective or words affect the outcome?

Facing difficult times can obscure the blessings waiting on the other side. How can you practice maintaining a positive outlook to help you navigate through these periods?

How might your words and thoughts act as a bridge to overcoming challenges and reaching the blessings God has prepared for you?

Engage the Master

*But seek first his kingdom and his righteousness, and all
these things will be given to you as well.*

—Matthew 6:33 (NIV)

^{1} *I lift up my eyes to the mountains—*
where does my help come from?
^{2} *My help comes from the Lord,*
the Maker of heaven and earth.

—Psalm 121:1-2 (NIV)

While on a recent trip, my wife attempted to turn the lights
on in our hotel room. There was a set of lights to the left,
and a single light to the right that was denoted "master"
above the switch. She switched all the lights on the left to
on, soon discovering that no lights were working. She looked
at me and said, "Why are the lights not working?" I said, "You
can have all of switches on the left on, but if the Master is
not engaged, none will work."

That is the story for many believers. We have attempted
to engage in certain things only to discover that everything
we have tried seems unsuccessful. Every recommendation,
every resource, and every effort have been explored, yet they
all prove futile. We are often left asking the question, "Why is
this not working?" "Why is this not happening for me?" In a
real sense, the answer is not out of reach. The lack of success
is not the result of a lack of effort but a failure to engage the
Master. If we are honest, it is fairly easy to go about things independently of God. However, we must realize that without
God, we can do nothing, but with God, there is nothing we

cannot do. When God controls something, it is impossible to be out of control. Whatever life pursuits are before you, do not forget to engage the Master.

Talk to Me God

How can you engage with God first in your daily activities and decisions? What practical steps can you take to prioritize His guidance above all else?

Reflect and Act: What current situation or decision could benefit from 'engaging the Master'? By 'engaging the Master, 'we mean seeking God's guidance and wisdom.

I Got Next

17 *I love those who love me, and those who seek me find me.* 18 *With me are riches and honor, enduring wealth, and prosperity.* 19 *My fruit is better than fine gold; what I yield surpasses choice silver.*

—*Proverbs 8:17-19 (NIV)*

When playing basketball or cards with my friends, there is a phrase that is consistent with both activities. "I got down." When a game is already in progress, and someone wants to participate in the next game, he says, "I got down," to let everyone know that he is next in line for the next game. After he declares, "I got down," he waits patiently for his turn to play.

In life, sometimes it may seem as if everyone around you is prospering in the very areas of life that you desire prosperity or simply forward progress. Everything seems to be happening for them, and nothing is happening for you. Everyone else is receiving or achieving the very things you desire, except you! When this occurs in your realm of friends and associates, it is easy to subconsciously become envious of the things people are experiencing around you if you are not careful. You can even become disgruntled with God because you feel God has abandoned you. Tony Gaskins once said, "There is no need to be jealous of others. What's for you is for you. And what they have wouldn't fit for you anyway. Be thankful for all you have and know that all you desire is coming." Therefore, when you witness others experiencing great things in life, I encourage you to look towards Heaven, put your hand up, and declare, "I got next". In the words of

Bishop TD Jakes, "God is not preparing the blessing for you; God is preparing you for the blessing!"

Talk to Me God

What can you do to prepare yourself for the blessings you believe are coming your way? How can focusing on your journey, rather than comparing it to others, help you remain positive and patient?

Next time you feel envious or impatient about your progress, remember to affirm, "I got next," trusting that God has a unique plan and timing for your life. What steps can you take to better prepare for your 'next'?

The Testimony of Your Scars

Let the redeemed of the Lord tell their story...

—*Psalm 107:2 (NIV)*

On yet another hot summer day in Memphis, I told my son Timothy to get dressed for the day. He went to his room and put on pants and a short-sleeved shirt. When I saw him, I suggested that he put some shorts on because he would be hot in the summer. My son sheepishly began to confess his hesitancy to wear shorts because of the scars on his legs. He was uncomfortable about the scars, which is why he preferred to wear pants so he could keep them covered. Already having shorts on, I threw my leg onto the bed and began to show him the scars on my legs he never paid attention to. It was amazing to see how he lit up, seeing that he was not alone in having some scars. My scars told him that you can live free and comfortable with some scars.

Too often in life, many people live in shame about what they have done or overcame. The truth is that we all have overcome some things and have some skeletons we hope never fall out of the closet. The Bible is replete of people with stories that pale in comparison to our worse deeds. Nevertheless, we tend to hide our scars rather than use our scars to help other people by sharing our testimonies. One writer said, "Your testimony is the greatest gift you can give to someone." In the story above, I was able to free my son from a self-imposed prison of shame by simply showing him and speaking of my scars. Obviously, I don't know what you have been through and certainly cannot speak of its impact on your life, but I do know that scars are different from wounds.

Scars are evidence of where you have been hurt but are now healed. Sharing your testimony is an act of faith that can bring hope and healing to others if you have the courage to make your scars public. God has chosen you to make a difference, and the testimony of your scars has the power to set someone free

Talk to Me God

Have you ever felt ashamed of your past experiences or mistakes? How might sharing your story help someone else going through something similar?

How can you embrace your scars as signs of healing and growth rather than sources of shame? What steps can you take to use your testimony to encourage and support others?

Think of one person who might benefit from hearing your story. Plan a way to share your testimony with them, knowing it could bring hope and healing.

The Costume Party of Life

*"And we pray this in order that you may live a life worthy
of the Lord and may please him in every way: bearing fruit
in every good work, growing in the knowledge of God,"*

—*Colossians 1:10 (NIV)*

Have you ever attended a costume party? Everyone wears
their masks and adorns themselves in attire characteristic of
the costume character. As one socializes at the party, one way
to determine who is behind the mask is by the person's voice.
Once the person begins to talk, you can determine by the
tone of their voice, what they say, and the topic of their conversation. The ability to recognize voices is one of the keys to
finding out who people are at a costume party.

Every day we live, we live the life of a costume party. Everyone looks a particular way and adorns themselves in attire
characteristic of their personality. As one socializes in life, we
find that many people look great, but we discern something
not quite right about them. The key to recognizing God's
people is not by how a person looks but by listening to the
soundtrack of their character. The tracks of a soundtrack of
character may include the audible voice that can be heard,
and the voice that can be seen. Today, we must ask ourselves,
"Do I live godly or just appear godly?" Mahatma Gandhi
summed it up, "An ounce of practice is worth more than tons
of preaching."

Talk to Me God

Reflect on a time when you realized someone was not who they appeared to be. How did their words or actions reveal their true character?

How can you ensure that your actions and words reflect a godly character, rather than just looking the part? What changes might you need to make to align more closely with your true values?

Clean Your System

"3 For though we walk in the flesh, we do not war according to the flesh. 4 For the weapons of our warfare are not carnal but mighty in God for pulling down strongholds, 5 casting down arguments and every high thing that exalts itself against the knowledge of God, bringing every thought into captivity to the obedience of Christ,"

—*2 Corinthians 10:3-5 (NKJV)*

Many of us use a computer at work or home. There are two things that are consistent with every computer system. Every system has both enter and delete buttons. The enter button confirms things we want to keep, and the delete button removes the characters we do not want or should not keep. If one is not careful and presses enter to keep everything, eventually, the system becomes cluttered and functions slowly. Therefore, it is recommended that the user occasionally check the system to see if there are items that could be deleted. When one deletes unnecessary items, they free up space for storing new things.

With everything that comes your way, you have two decisions to make. You can decide to accept it (enter) or reject it (delete). Many people are functioning slowly in the Christian walk because they have pressed *enter* on some things they should have deleted. Some pressed 'enter' to people telling them they can't. Some have pressed 'enter' to people telling them they are unattractive. Some have pressed 'enter' to the negative opinions of others concerning them. As people of God, we must take inventory of ourselves and determine if some things need deletion. Today, clean your system! To create space for new things, you must let go of the things and people no longer serving you well. Delete every negative thought, opinion, attitude, or situation that rises so you can free up space for the new things God has in store for you.

Talk to Me God

What negative thoughts or opinions have you held onto that might be slowing you down? How can you "delete" these from your mind and make room for positive changes?

How can you regularly inventory your thoughts and beliefs to keep what's helpful and delete what's harmful? What steps can you take today to start this process?

Identify one negative belief or thought you frequently "enter" into your mind. Commit to actively deleting and replacing it with a positive, affirming thought.

Have a Clearance Sale

"Brothers, I do not consider myself yet to have taken hold of it. But one thing I do: Forgetting what is behind and straining toward what is ahead,"

—Philippians 3:13 (NIV)

The clearance rack is the first rack many people (like me) go to when shopping. Most large stores typically have a clearance rack. This rack is for the items the store desires to sell, but the items are inhibiting new items from being able to go on the rack. In an effort to make room, store management is willing to do whatever it takes to get customers to purchase the items. One week, everything might be 25% off, then 50% off the next week, and 60% off the week after that. In short, the store does whatever it takes to get the items out of the way. If the store attempted to maintain the old items in addition to the new, a cluttered store would result. Therefore, to prevent this occurrence, store management decides to get rid of old items by any means necessary. All transactions are typically final, accompanied by the inability to exchange.

What are you holding on to? You may be hanging on to things that happened many years ago. Someone hurt you a long time ago, and you haven't spoken to them since? Someone made a statement, and you concluded you were never going back? Maybe there is something else you are harboring toward a family member, friend, associate, or maybe a church member. The truth is that if you do not authentically release the grudges, your heart and mind will become cluttered with resentment and negativity. The resentment and negativity on the rack of your heart inhibit the new things God desires

67

to do in your life. You cannot hold on to the old and hope to have a new one in the future. Have a clearance sale! Get rid of the anger, regret, worry, resentment, guilt, and even blame, and watch how your life improves.

Talk to Me God

Is there something from your past that you're holding on to, like anger or regret? How can letting go of this "old item" make room for new blessings in your life?

What steps can you take to clear out negative emotions or grudges? How might this create a more positive and open space for God's new plans for you?

A Back-Stage Pass

"Above all else, guard your heart, for it is the wellspring of life."

—*Proverbs 4:23 (NIV)*

When it comes to concerts, many attendees desire to have a backstage pass. Having a back-stage pass allows the attendees to experience more than other people who attend the concert. The backstage gives the privilege to see and talk to the artists up close and personal. To obtain the pass, one must go through a thorough check to ensure that no harm would be done to the artists by the attendee. It is known that not every attendee has good intentions, so the examination must be done. After the concert, security ensures that only those holding a backstage pass gain access to the artists.

When it comes to people in your life, perform a thorough *check* before you issue a backstage pass to your heart. People who are close to your heart have an opportunity to see and talk to you up close and personal. They know your likes, dislikes, pains, and triumphs. They have a different experience with you than others. They have a backstage pass. It is important to note that not everyone who comes into your life has good intentions. Therefore, each person (even those you meet in church) who comes into your life should be thoroughly examined with prayer and discernment. Only those who pass the Spirit's security check and approval should you issue a backstage pass. The failure to do this can cause you to give basement people top-tier access to your life.

Talk to Me God

Have you ever given someone access to your heart who didn't have the best intentions? Reflecting on this experience is crucial for protecting your emotional well-being.

How can you use discernment to decide who should have a "backstage pass" to your life? What steps can you take to protect your heart and ensure only trustworthy people get close? Remember, discernment is your superpower.

Think of someone in your life who might not have the best intentions. Pray for discernment and set firm boundaries to guard your heart. These boundaries are your shield, protecting you from harm.

God Is Still in Control

"2 Grace and peace be yours in abundance through the knowledge of God and of Jesus our Lord. 3 His divine power has given us everything we need for life and godliness through our knowledge of him, who called us by his own glory and goodness. 4 Through these, he has given us his very great and precious promises, so that through them you may participate in the divine nature and escape the corruption in the world caused by evil desires."

—2 Peter 1:2-4 (NIV)

Today's technology makes it seem as if a button controls everything. Technology allows us to scan viruses on our computers to prevent them from crashing. Technology allows us to be on the Internet and prevent missing phone calls. Technology allows us to receive vaccinations to prevent the flu and other illnesses. The list can go on and on about how technology allows us to stop or lessen the likelihood of something happening, and many people depend on it in many areas of life.

A tremendous storm hit our city some time ago that left trees uprooted and thousands of people without power cable and phone access. Although technology was able to predict the storm's coming, it could not prevent the storm from occurring. This was a simple reminder that anything that seems out of control is still under God's control. Technology and human genius can only take us to a certain point. When faced with a problem, many people resort to consultations with professionals, information from books, or the Internet, and they rely on the given information for what they need.

While it is good to be knowledgeable and informed, it is vital that we (the people of God) rely on God for the solutions to our issues and concerns rather than technology or human genius. The search engine can provide information, but only the Savior can provide the solution. Remember this...God can do a lot more with your surrender than you can with your control.

Talk to Me God

How can you replace reliance on human inventions with trusting in God's power and promises? What are some actual, practical steps that can be made toward deepening your belief in God's control over every aspect of your life?

The next time you face a problem, pause to pray and offer it to God. Observe how that act of faith changes your perspective and brings peace.

Just Send It

"Whenever you are arrested and brought to trial, do not worry beforehand about what to say. Just say whatever is given you at the time, for it is not you speaking, but the Holy Spirit."

—*Mark 13:11 (NIV)*

One of my favorite hobbies is dining at different restaurants and trying a variety of entrees and appetizers. Although I have eaten at many different restaurants, meeting the chef face-to-face is something that seldom happens. Often, the most knowledge I have about the cook is whether the food was good or not simply based on my experience. The cook's responsibility is to prepare and send food to my table, they NEVER make sure I clean the plate by eating all the food. The cook sends it, and it is my choice to consume it.

As children of God, we serve as God's proverbial cook for someone people around us. God gives us an *order* to say or do something for someone we know or may not know. Oftentimes, we do not understand why, when, or how we are to do what God asks us to do. However, as God's *cook*, it is our responsibility to simply send the order to the table of that person's heart. After we do/say what God has commanded, it is their choice to receive it. Often, we want to 'witness' the results of our actions for ourselves, meaning we want to see the immediate impact of our obedience. Nevertheless, we must be reminded that our responsibility is to fulfill God's order and not make sure the person cleans the plate by receiving what God has served. The next time God time gives us an order to fulfill, do not ask questions, do not delay, just send it.

Maybe there is something that has been on your heart to do or say that you have delayed, consider this devotional as your confirmation. Do it today.

Talk to Me God

Have you ever felt prompted by God to say or do something for someone but hesitated because you wanted to see the results? How can you trust your obedience is enough, even if you don't see the immediate impact?

Is there something you feel God has been asking you to do or say but you've been delaying? How can you take a step today to "just send it" and trust that God will handle the rest?

Your Daddy Did It

[16] So don't be misled, my dear brothers and sisters. [17] Whatever is good and perfect is a gift coming down to us from God our Father, who created all the lights in the heavens. He never changes or casts a shifting shadow.

—James 1:16-17 (NLT)

[1] I will give thanks to you, Lord, with all my heart;
* I will tell of all your wonderful deeds.*
[2] I will be glad and rejoice in you;
* I will sing the praises of your name, O Most High.*

—Psalm 9:1-2

Years ago, the family and I were at the bowling alley with some friends and their children. All of our children were fairly small, so the adults were helping the kids bowl. During the first game, I was primarily helping my son. After the game, he stood as the winner of the kid's game. Witnessing him brag about the strikes *he* got and how *he* won the game was comical. Interestingly, he seemed to conveniently forget that his daddy helped him along the way, and he won solely because of his father.

My friend, when it comes to the successes, accomplishments, and achievements in our lives, it can be tempting to have a posture that suggests we accomplished them in our own power. This is a dangerous posture for the believer because it is a posture of accepting credit for what we could not have done without the Father's provision and assistance. Manny Pacquiao once said, "Even in my prime, I need God in my life because, without God, we're nothing." Pacquiao's

75

words are true for all of us as believers. It is vital that we never get so excited about our victories in life that we forget to remember and acknowledge the fact that it is solely because of the Father that victory was achieved in lieu of defeat. Today, think about all God has blessed you with and all that He has allowed you to accomplish, and tell the world over that it was not because of your intelligence, connections, or self-will, but simply because your daddy did it!

Talk to Me God

Think of a time you did not thank God for success. What would you do so that you remember His assistance more often?

Share a story of God's help in your success. What will this do for your faith and the faith of others?

Give It Your All

"David and all the Israelites were celebrating with all their might before God, with songs and with harps, lyres, tambourines, cymbals and trumpets."

—*1 Chronicles 13:8 (NIV)*

"So, whether you eat or drink or whatever you do, do it all for the glory of God."

—*1 Corinthians 10:31 (NIV)*

In the sports world, every good player always wants to play for a good coach. A good coach typically brings out the best in each player. A good player always wants to play well for a good coach. A good player gives his all in everything—in practice, warm-ups, games, and the classroom. This is consistent with every sport; players want to perform according to the coach's theme, "Give it all you got!"

As the children of God, we have the greatest Coach! We have a Coach greater than any coach in the NBA, NFL, NHL, or MLB! As God's star players, we should want to play the game of life well in order to please God. Knowing that we have the greatest Coach, we should give our all in whatever we do. Teaching? Give it your all! Speaking? Give it your all! Singing? Give it your all! Cleaning up? Give it your all! Cooking? Give it your all! Working? Give it your all! Rick Warren concludes, "Work becomes worship when you dedicate it to God and perform it with an awareness of His presence." Whatever you put your hands to, give it your all—do it all for the glory of God.

Talk to Me God

Think of a task or activity you often do. How can you start giving it your all for God's glory?

Imagine your work to worship God. How can this perspective change the way you approach your daily tasks?

Pick one thing you do today and give it your all, dedicating it to God. Notice how this effort makes you feel and share your experience with someone.

A Spiritual Physical

"Examine yourselves to see whether you are in the faith; test yourselves. Do you not realize that Christ Jesus is in you–unless, of course, you fail the test?"

—*2 Corinthians 13:5 (NIV)*

To maintain a healthy lifestyle, one should get an annual physical as recommended. This is in addition to the personal examinations that should be performed throughout the year. During the physical, the doctor checks the body for blood pressure, diseases, infections, and various other things. One should get a physical annually because things can change in a person's body yearly. Therefore, it is necessary to get checked to ensure that all is well.

In the Christian walk, it is necessary that we take a spiritual physical. In the spiritual physical, we should use the Word of God to check for unconfessed sin, sinful habits, infectious relationships, unforgiveness, and other things. If anything is found in our lives, it is important that we seek the Doctor to obtain the necessary treatment or prescription. This physical is needed daily to ensure a spiritually healthy lifestyle. With a thorough physical, things are revealed that are not detectable from outside appearance. "God, as we examine our lives, show us anything/anyone that is not in your will for our lives. We seek you for the treatment/prescription to remove them from our lives so that we can be spiritually healthy. Give us the courage to do or say whatever you prescribe for our situations. In Jesus' name, we pray, Amen!"

Talk to Me God

How can regularly examining your spiritual life help you stay aligned with God's will? What steps can you take to start this practice?

Take a moment today to reflect on your spiritual health. Pray for guidance and ask God to reveal areas that need attention.

No Vacancy

"⁶ Don't worry about anything, but pray about everything. With thankful hearts, offer up your prayers and requests to God. ⁷ Then, because you belong to Christ Jesus, God will bless you with peace that no one can completely understand. And this peace will control the way you think and feel."

—*Philippians 4:6-7 (CEV)*

Before modern technology paved the way for online hotel bookings, have you ever gone to a hotel and been welcomed by a "no vacancy" sign? You and your family are in need of rest, only to be disappointed by this sign. It plainly tells us, "All of our rooms are occupied. You have no reason for you to enter because we have no room for you." After reading the sign, it becomes necessary to move on, seeking accommodation elsewhere.

As the people of God, we must keep the Word of God in our hearts and lips. If we do this, all areas of our lives will be occupied with godly things/thoughts rather than worldly things/thoughts. We should keep our families, jobs, relationships, ministries, and other areas lifted in prayer. Doing this prepares us for when we are next on the devil's list. When he arrives, we can simply tell him, "All areas are occupied, there is no room for you." It then becomes necessary for the devil to go back to where he came from. We must stay prayed up, so the next time the enemy comes to attack us, we can tell him, "No Vacancy!"

Talk to Me God

Reflect on areas of your life where negative thoughts or influences might try to enter. How can you keep these areas "occupied" with godly thoughts and prayers?

What daily practices can you implement to ensure that your heart and mind remain focused on God, leaving no room for negativity or doubt?

Live In Your Habitat

"Do not let this Book of the Law depart from your mouth;
meditate on it day and night so that you may be careful to
do everything written in it. Then you will be prosperous
and successful."

—*Joshua 1:8 (NIV)*

There are several kinds of fish that many of us enjoy eating. Whiting, bass, buffalo, bream, and, most of all, catfish are a few we enjoy the most. The one thing that all fish have in common is that they are all created to live in water. Outside of water, fish struggle to breathe and eventually die. They can survive only for a brief period outside of their habitat. Therefore, fish are created to depend on water for their survival.

We are created to depend on the Word of God for our survival. When we fail to have quiet time with God and spend time in His Word, we find ourselves struggling in various areas of life. We find ourselves struggling to maintain the right attitude at work/home. We find ourselves falling to temptation. We find ourselves doing old things with old people and going back to old places. The Word of God is our habitat, and we are created to depend on it for survival. Outside of the Word of God, a spiritual death will eventually occur, and we will return to our old way of life. Therefore, we must live in our habitat by meditating on the Word every day, every hour, every minute, and every second to survive.

Talk to Me God

How does spending time in God's Word help you stay strong and focused in your daily life? What happens when you neglect this habit?

What steps can you take to meditate on God's Word regularly? How can making this a daily practice improve your spiritual health?

Double-Dutch

"¹ Praise the LORD. Blessed is the man who fears the LORD, who finds great delight in his commands. ² His children will be mighty in the land; the generation of the upright will be blessed. ³ Wealth and riches are in his house, and his righteousness endures forever."

—Psalm 112:1-3 (NIV)

Growing up, the girls in our community loved to double-Dutch jump rope. Two people would hold two ropes and turn them simultaneously for the jumper. I would get a kick out of watching the jumper as she hesitated before jumping into the ropes. She would lean back and forth, carefully watching the ropes as they turned, and finally hop in and begin jumping. Timing was the key to double-Dutch jump rope.

Sometimes in life, it can seem that everything and everyone is turning on and around us. It seems that everyone around you is prospering. It seems that nothing else can go wrong in your life. It seems that your supervisor suddenly has something against you. Your money has suddenly gotten funny. Maybe some other situation has you down. My friend, the ropes are turning! Child of God, be encouraged. God is watching the ropes turn in your life, carefully watching from nearby, and will jump into your situation. As your life seems to be in a state of double-Dutch, know that God is about to jump in and bless you beyond your imagination!

Talk to Me God

Reflect on one of those times when everything seemed to be falling apart in your life. How did you perceive God's intervention, guiding you through it?

How do you hold on to the belief in God's perfect timing, especially when life's challenges seem never-ending and overwhelming?

Blind Seven

"For we walk by faith, not by sight"

—2 Corinthians 5:7 (KJV)

While playing the card game Spades, my partner and I found ourselves in dire need of points. It seemed that no matter what we did to accumulate books, nothing seemed to work. When all hope seemed to be lost, my partner and I decided to go blind seven. Blind seven is when a team proclaims they will win seven books before the cards are even dealt. Going blind seven is a huge gamble because one doesn't know what kind of hand they will have when dealing with the cards. However, the points are doubled if the team achieves the seven books they declared they would win. When a team is significantly behind, it can be beneficial to go blind seven.

At this point in your life, do you need something in particular? Encouragement? Financial increase? Employment? Something else? Of course, there are a number of things that could be added to the list of needs. Interestingly, but equally frustrating, is that there are times when you are doing everything you can to achieve some measure of progress, but it seems nothing seems to work no matter what you do. In short, your fruit does not match your efforts. Today, go blind seven. What does that mean? Speak and proclaim receipt and victory now before your situation is resolved. You have to speak faith despite the facts. Be so confident in the Hand of God, knowing that God already knows the outcome, and the outcome is in your favor! When things seem to get worse rather than better, determining blind seven with God (your Partner) will ultimately double your progress of blessing.

Talk to Me God

How can trusting in God's plan and proclaiming victory now, before seeing the results, change your perspective and give you hope

Identify a current need in your life. Speak words of faith and trust in God's plan, believing that He will provide what you need. Share this practice of faith with someone who might need encouragement.

Upside Down

"²Consider it pure joy, my brothers, whenever you face trials of many kinds, ³because you know that the testing of your faith develops perseverance. ⁴Perseverance must finish its work so that you may be mature and complete, not lacking anything."

—James 1:2-4 (NIV)

One day, after preparing dinner, I went to the pantry only to find the ketchup with only a little remaining in the bottle. I really wanted the ketchup for my gourmet fish and fries dinner! What did I do? I simply turned the bottle upside down to get out the little bit of ketchup that was left in the bottle. I was determined to do everything I could out of it, even if it meant leaving the bottle upside down for a period. With the bottle turned upside down, I waited until all the contents migrated to the inverted top to get what I wanted.

One common misconception is that life in God is all sunshine and rainbows. Nevertheless, after a while, the Christian discovers that trouble and difficulty land in the lives of believers. Life can literally turn upside down. One moment, things are fine, and the next moment, things are falling apart. One day, you have money, and one repair need can siphon the preponderance of that money away. One day, the marriage is wonderful; the next day, it is horrible. One day, you are healthy, and one trip to the doctor's office can turn your life upside down! During these times, you wonder, "Lord, what is going on? Why me?" My friend, when your life seems to turn upside down, know that it is the perfect opportunity for God to get out of you all that God desires to get out of you.

God desires to get trust out of you. God desires to get more faith out of you. God desires more hope from you. God is determined to get out of you what is inside you, but your life has to be turned upside down for it to happen. During this season in your life, know that God is bringing out what is already in you because God needs what's in you for what God has prepared.

Talk to Me God

When have you felt like your life was turned upside down? How did those problematic times bring out qualities like faith, trust, or hope in you?

How can you see your current struggles as opportunities for God to bring out the best in you? What can you learn from these experiences?

It's on the Books

"For I know the plans I have for you," declares the LORD, "plans to prosper you and not to harm you, plans to give you hope and a future."

—*Jeremiah 29:11 (NIV)*

When a person is incarcerated, their family and friends can deposit money into their account, commonly referred to as "putting money on the books." This money allows inmates to purchase necessities and some comforts. Although money is available to the inmate, security is in place to ensure that the money is not used to buy something illegal or something that would harm them.

We often hear the saying, "Ask and you shall receive; knock and the door will be opened." We have the faith to know that God is able and can provide ALL things. However, for some of us, it seems that God is not giving us what we are asking for. When we ask, and God seems to be silent, we begin to wonder if what we are asking for is "on the books." We must know that although God has many blessings on the books, God will not give us what God feels we cannot handle or would be detrimental to us. God is determined to protect us, and God knows what is best for us. God's best is on the books for you!

Talk to Me God

Have you ever asked God for something and felt like you didn't get an answer? How can trusting that God knows what is best for you change your perspective on unanswered prayers?

What blessings or opportunities might God be preparing for you that you can't see yet? How can you remain patient and faithful while waiting for God's timing?

Please Buzz Me In

"Not everyone who says to me, 'Lord, Lord,' will enter the kingdom of heaven, but only he who does the will of my Father who is in heaven."

—*Matthew 7:21 (NIV)*

The company I work for has very stringent security measures. Practically everywhere one goes, one has to be buzzed in after being identified as an employee of the company. While traveling to another state, I went to my company's office building. When I arrived at the door, I looked at the receptionist with a look of "please, buzz me in!" Of course, if I were not an employee of the company, she would have left me standing outside of where I wanted to be.

The people of God have a standard by which we are to live. Each day, choices must be made–this way or that way, right or wrong, God's will or my will, and the list goes on. However, it is imperative that we follow God's measures for life so that when judgment day comes, He will buzz us in. If we are not walking and doing the things God has asked of us, we will be left standing and crying outside of where we all want to be. Every day we live, let us strive to follow God's Word in all that what we do and say. If we do this, when we reach the gates of Heaven, we will be recognized by the great Receptionist, and He will buzz us in with the words we all hope to hear, "Servant well done!"

Talk to Me God

Think about the choices you make each day. Are they in line with God's will? How can you ensure you're living in a way that pleases Him?

How can you incorporate more of God's Word into your daily life to be sure you're following His standards? What small changes can you start making today?

Trash or Recycle

"Therefore, since we are surrounded by such a great cloud of witnesses, let us throw off everything that hinders and the sin that so easily entangles, and let us run with perseverance the race marked out for us."

—*Hebrews 12:1 (NIV)*

While on a business trip to Minneapolis, MN, I had the opportunity to visit the Mall of America. Throughout the mall, there are waste bins and recycle bins strategically placed on each floor. The bins are located side by side, leaving it up to the consumer to determine what to place in each bin. Management sometimes becomes irritated when consumers place trash in the recycle bin when it should go in the trash bin and vice versa.

As you grow in your relationship with God, God sometimes calls you away from some people and things. When God calls you away, God maintains a hopeful expectation that you will not return. Nevertheless, because we are sinful humanity, you and I have the tendency to recycle that which God told you to trash. As flawed humans, we sometimes recycle old ways of thinking and old ways of doing things, and even old places. As flawed humans, we sometimes recycle old and harmful relationships God has called us out of. Today, examine your life and assess whether God could be irritated because you are choosing to recycle what God told you to trash. Trash or recycle?

Talk to Me God

Are there old habits or relationships that God has called you away from but you keep returning to? How can you start letting go of these things for good?

How can you better discern what to trash and what to recycle in your life? What steps can you take to follow God's guidance more closely?

Take a moment to identify something in your life that God may want you to let go of. Pray for strength to "trash" it and not recycle it. Share this decision with someone who can support you.

On Occasion?

> [1] *I will bless the LORD at all times: His praise shall* *continually be in my mouth.* [2] *My soul shall make her boast* *in the LORD: the humble shall hear thereof, and be **glad**.*
>
> —*Psalm 34:1-2 (KJV)*

"On occasion" is a common response to a variety of questions. When one is asked, do you drink alcohol? The response may be "on occasion". Do you go smoke cigarettes? "On occasion." "Do you go to the club? "On occasion." These two words suggest that whatever we are speaking of is not something that one does all the time but rather something we do every now and then–just on occasion.

As we continue to grow in our relationship with God, we must be careful that we do not praise and worship God just on occasion. When the bank account is favorable, that's an acceptable occasion. When all is well in the workplace, that's an occasion. When the children are doing well and things are good at home, that's an occasion. This should not be the posture of a believer because in every season of life, God is still good. Rick Warren once said, "Praise is the evidence of faith. If you believe that God is good and that He loves you, then you will praise Him in every season of your life." We should praise and worship God in both the good and tough times, in pain and suffering, in times of prosperity and welfare, in moments of uncertainty, and through all other circumstances. The expectation is to praise God at ALL times, not just on occasion.

Talk to Me God

Do you find yourself only praising God during good times? How can you start praising Him in all circumstances, both good and bad?

How can you make praising and worshipping God a regular part of your daily life rather than something you do only occasionally?

Stay At the Bus Stop

"May the LORD, the God of your fathers, increase you a thousand times and bless you as he has promised!"

—*Deuteronomy 1:11 (NIV)*

One day, my mind reflected on the days in which I rode the bus to and from my first job. I remember standing at the bus stop waiting on my bus, the #11 bus. I was always advised to get to the bus stop before the scheduled time of arrival. I waited alongside several people at the bus stop. I would often get impatient as I stood in admiration of others as they boarded their buses. Hot, frustrated, and irritated, I wanted *my* bus to come on *my* schedule, not the MATA (Memphis Area Transit Authority) schedule. To my dismay, the #11 bus never came on *my* schedule, but it always arrived on a schedule that was determined by someone who was above me.

Many of us are waiting on something from God. Alongside friends, family, and associates, you are standing at the bus stop of blessing, patiently waiting for its arrival. Some are waiting on the relationship or marriage bus. Others are waiting on the financial blessing bus. Some are waiting on the healing bus. Obviously, the list of buses is endless, but the reality is that everyone is waiting for something from God. If you are honest, sometimes your patience can run thin in the process. It is especially bothersome when you have to watch others board their bus of blessing while you wait for you. However, this can be bothersome and even discouraging to a degree. Patience to wait on God's timing does not come easy. It is a conscious decision to wait well and be reminded of the fact God is not on your schedule but always on His. God has perfect timing, never early and never late. Waiting takes patience and a lot of faith, but it's well worth the wait. In the meantime, stay at the bus stop!

Talk to Me God

Are you waiting for a blessing from God and feeling impatient? How can you remind yourself that God's timing is perfect, even when it doesn't match your schedule?

How can you practice patience and faith while waiting for God's blessings? What can you do to stay encouraged during this waiting period?

Close the Door Behind You

¹³... But one thing I do: Forgetting what is behind and straining toward what is ahead, ¹⁴I press on toward the goal to win the prize for which God has called me heavenward in Christ Jesus.

—*Philippians 3:13-14 (NIV)*

Anyone who lives or has visited the South knows that it gets extremely hot during the summer season! The humidity in the South is unbelievable compared to other areas of the country. Because our home had no garage while I was growing up, we put extra effort into ensuring the door was shut immediately after entering the house. When we would walk inside the house, my mom would say, "Make sure you shut the door all the way." The goal was to keep the hot air outside as we enjoy the comfort of air conditioning on the inside. If the door was not shut immediately and completely, the inside of our house could become as hot and uncomfortable as the heat outside.

This is the season to shut the door behind you. Sometimes, you can find yourself dwelling on what you should have done, could have done, or did not do. Dwelling on the past is nothing short of unproductive. Therefore, it is important that we shut the door to the past immediately and completely to move forward. If we do not do this, we will find ourselves miserable and hesitant about moving forward, attempting, and doing new things. Now that you are on the inside, having a relationship with God when you think about your past, make sure that you have closed the door behind you. Once you realize the bright future God has for you, you will discover that letting go of your past is the best decision you will ever make. Close the door behind you!

Talk to Me God

Are you holding on to past mistakes or regrets? How can letting go of the past help you move forward and embrace the future God has for you?

How can you practice closing the door on negative past experiences and focus on the new opportunities ahead? What steps can you take today to start this process?

Identify something from your past that you're holding on to. Pray for the strength to let it go and focus on the future.

The Ultimate Bargain

For God so loved the world that he gave his one and only Son, that whoever believes in him shall not perish but have eternal life.

—John 3:16 (NIV)

It runs well, like new, many new parts, is still in boxes, is clean, has one owner, and is beautiful are descriptive words often used to advertise goods available for sale. In each ad, the seller attempts to market the item and describe it as best as they can to encourage people to buy something even without seeing it. Often, one may see the price preceded by the words *motivated seller*. This notation suggests that the price offered to the buyer is certainly a bargain compared to what he/she paid.

It is amazing how Jesus remains in the classified section, and many people have not accepted Jesus yet. There is but One Owner of humanity who is clean, beautiful, runs well and offers newness of life along with a lifetime warranty. The price of confession and belief in the death, burial, and resurrection of Jesus is a tremendous bargain compared to the price God paid for us. God sold His Son to us at the ultimate price. The least we can do is encourage others to buy into Him (even without physically seeing Him) by giving their lives to Him. So often, we take the sacrifice of Jesus for granted, but ultimately, the Calvary transaction was and remains the ultimate bargain for humanity.

Talk to Me God

Have you accepted the ultimate bargain of Jesus' sacrifice? How does this understanding change your perspective on God's love for you?

How can you share the message of Jesus' ultimate bargain with others who may not know Him yet? What steps can you take to encourage others to believe in Him?

God Cleaned Your Mess

On that day tell your son, 'I do this because of what the LORD did for me when I came out of Egypt.'

—*Exodus 13:8 (NIV)*

Have you ever been in a situation where you felt as if you were always cleaning up others' messes? You found yourself doing things they were tasked to do. You were assigned to complete things the other person(s) should have done a long time ago. Overtime was required of you because you had to devote some of your time doing someone else's job. Sound familiar? One may relate to these things on the job, in school projects, and even in church ministry. Truthfully, there are times you want to verbalize what is in your mind/heart—"I am tired of cleaning your mess and doing what you are supposed to do!"

While most can relate to the examples above, have you ever stopped to consider how often God cleaned your mess? Have you had situations in your lives where God had to step in and clean up what you messed up? In fact, God had someone else do what you were asked to do, but you didn't do it. Maybe God tasked someone else to complete what God told you to do a long time ago. The list goes on and on about how many times God had to clean your mess. Today, you may be irritated and frustrated performing someone else's job or responsibilities at work, school, church, or some other entity. Although it may be difficult to do, be thankful for the fact that God cleaned your mess.

Talk to Me God

Think about times when God stepped in to fix your mistakes. How can remembering these moments help you be more patient when you're cleaning up someone else's mess?

How can you show gratitude to God for the times He has helped you? What can you do to extend that grace to others in your life?

It's All Good

And we know that in ALL things, God works for the good of those who love Him, who have been called according to his purpose.

—Romans 8:28 (NIV)

As a child, I abhorred eating Raisin Bran cereal! The cereal was naturally sweetened with raisins but not sweet enough for my sweet tooth. I was always aware that the cereal was good for me. I would try to add a little sugar, but the sugar would just go to the bottom of the bowl. Ultimately, no matter what I did to Raisin Bran, it just didn't taste good! As the years passed, I discovered the magnificent world of Trix, Fruit Loops, Honeycomb, and others! These cereals were good for the taste buds but not as healthy as Raisin Bran for the body. In many areas of life, including my choice of cereal, I've come to realize that sometimes things that are good *to* me are not necessarily good *for* me. Conversely, sometimes things that don't seem good to you are actually beneficial.

I believe it is safe to say that you have experienced situations in life that were painful, discouraging, and troubling, among other things. Being hurt, losing a job, failing a class, family troubles, persecution, loss, and other things we experience simply do not taste good. During these times, you wished you could add a little 'sugar' to it to cause the experience to taste better, but all your efforts proved futile. Nevertheless, you later discovered that the situations that didn't taste good are the very situations that make you the person you are today. While the experiences didn't taste good *to* you, however, God made sure that it worked out well for you.

Surely, life without pain and difficulties would taste good to us. However, it is through the Raisin Bran situations that God takes you to higher levels in God. Ultimately, God's purpose will always be greater than your problems. When you are facing a situation that is not pleasing, God says to you today, it's ALL good!

Talk to Me God

How can you believe that God is working for your good, even when life doesn't "taste" good? What steps can you take to remain faithful during difficult times?

Think about a challenge you are facing at the moment. Remind yourself that there's no problem God can't use to work something good out. Think of the lessons and growth it will bring, and pause to thank Him for it.

Trust the Director

⁵ Trust in the LORD with all your heart and lean not on your own understanding;

⁶ in all your ways acknowledge him, and he will make your paths straight.

—Proverbs 3:5-6 (NIV)

One day, I watched a show about the special effects in music videos. In some videos, a green screen is used to create certain images or backgrounds. The artist performs in front of the blank green screen while the director adds the special effects. In the actual video and movie, the artist can be seen driving, walking by a lake, or some other special effect, when in reality, it was just a blank green screen. On the show, one artist spoke about how he just does what he is supposed to do in front of the green screen and trusts the director to make the image what it should be.

There are moments in life when you can feel like you don't have a clue about ANYTHING! You don't know whether you are coming or going. You have a blurred view of your future. You live each day wondering how things will turn out. You, my friend, are standing in front of the green screen. Life seems blank, unfulfilling, and uncertain. Let me encourage you. Although you may be standing in front of the green screen of life, there is a great Director behind the scenes creating special effects for your life. What looks blank to you is a great image for God to work with and add what God desires to add. As God crafts the finished product, you must do what you know you are to do and trust God as the Director. You may not know what the future holds, but be certain of Who holds the future.

Talk to Me God

Have you ever felt uncertain about your future? How can trusting God as the Director help you feel more at peace?

How can you focus on doing what you know is right while trusting God to handle the rest? What steps can you take to deepen your trust in Him?

Don't Settle for the Preview

Now to him who is able to do immeasurably more than all we ask or imagine, according to his power that is at work within us

—*Ephesians 3:20 (NIV)*

...I have come that they may have life and have it to the full.

—*John 10:10b (NIV)*

Before the modern days of online news sources, newspaper stands were common in various places, even at restaurants. I recall an occasion when I was in the drive-thru at McDonald's; there was a newspaper stand with the front page of the paper in the window of the stand. As I waited to order, I read the articles I could see in the window of the stand. When I reached the end of the article, there was a note at the bottom that said the article was "continued on G8." It was at that moment that I realized the genius of having a preview window on a newspaper stand. The purpose of having the front page in the window is to give you a preview of what is inside. Therefore, to receive all the paper had to offer, a purchase or sacrifice must be made. On that day, I decided not to settle for the preview.

My friend, you are blessed! Yes, I mean you! You are blessed! Take a moment to consider the physical, material, and spiritual blessings in your life. You may not have all that you want, but you certainly have all that you need. Despite how blessed you are, this is only a preview of what God ultimately has for you. As a child, I would often hear, "If God doesn't do anything else, He has already done enough." My friend, God wants you to know that it gets greater later. Though your current life may be good, it is just a preview. God wants to bless you abundantly. However, to get everything God has for you, you must submit completely to God and God's will for your life. Whatever you do, don't settle for the preview!

Talk to Me God

Reflect on the blessings you currently have. How can recognizing these as a preview inspire you to seek even more of what God has planned for you?

How can you come to a place of complete submission to God's will in your life in order to experience the abundance He has promised? What steps can you take beyond the preview in order to embrace all that God has for you?

Disconnected-Part I

[19] *For through the law I died to the law so that I might live for God.* [20] *I have been crucified with Christ and I no longer live, but Christ lives in me. The life I live in the body, I live by faith in the Son of God, who loved me and gave himself for me.*

—Galatians 2:19-20 (NIV)

After a while of non-communication, I attempted to call a friend of mine from high school. Rather than being greeted with a "hello," I was greeted with a noise followed by, 'The number you have dialed has been disconnected or is no longer in service; please check the number and dial again.' Thinking that I possibly pressed the wrong digit, I called again and was greeted with the same message.

After a while of living for Christ, Satan attempts to trip us up with the usual stuff he used to get us with. However, some of us are at a point where we have disconnected some areas of life, and those areas are no longer in service. The same voice doesn't affect us anymore. The same issues don't upset us anymore. The same difficulties don't frustrate us anymore. And the list goes on. Therefore, when Satan tries to call us up with old things/people, we can now say, "Satan, the number you have dialed has been disconnected AND is no longer in service; check the number and dial again; you will be greeted with the same message." Today, praise God that you have been disconnected from the old things that once had a hold on you!

Talk to Me God

Think about a habit or issue that has been conquered by faith. How will this reminder of growth in faith help you to stand firm against old temptations?

How do you manage to keep your disengagement from past struggles and keep on growing in faith? What means could you use to ensure that you stay "disconnected"?

Disconnected-Part II

⁵ He who overcomes will, like them, be dressed in white. I will never blot out his name from the book of life, but will acknowledge his name before my Father and his angels. ⁶He who has an ear, let him hear what the Spirit says to the churches.

—*Revelation 3:5-6 (NIV)*

After a while of non-communication, I attempted to call a friend from high school. Rather than being greeted with a "hello," I was greeted with a noise followed by, 'The number you have dialed (quote the number) has been changed to a non-published number.' It was not that the person no longer lived in Memphis or no longer lived in the same house. It was simply a change of phone number. The fact that the number was 'non-published' in the white pages signified that he only wanted certain people to have his number.

There was once a time when Satan could trip you up using a variety of things. However, at some point, you have a decision to seriously live for Christ and change your life. When Satan and even people began to witness your metamorphosis, they were incapable of understanding what was happening. Though your physical body and location remain unchanged, there are some undeniable changes prompted by God. Satan was forced to accept that you chose to remove your name from the white pages of damnation. Today is a good day to celebrate that you are not published on Satan's white pages, but God has your number, and it is listed in the Book of Life!

Talk to Me God

How have the changes in your life brought you closer to God? What is the most powerful change you have been able to make?

How do you keep reflecting on your growth in the journey of faith while being tempted or tested? What practical steps help you remain committed to Christ?

Don't Do It Alone

⁹ Two are better than one, because they have a good return for their labor: ¹⁰ If either of them falls down, one can help the other up. But pity anyone who falls and has no one to help them up.

—*Ecclesiastes 4:9-10 (NIV)*

My son Timothy and I enjoy watching shows related to animals and how they function. The uniqueness of spiders was featured on one show. Though neither of us is fond of spiders in our personal space, it was quite interesting to learn how some species of spiders collaborate. During the show, a gargantuan spider web was pictured. The narrator asserted that some species of spiders come together in the jungle to create a vast web that is capable of catching prey as large as birds, which individually woven webs are impotent in accomplishing.

Michael Jordan once said, "Talent wins games, but teamwork and intelligence win championships." When it comes to many things in life, it can be easy to adopt a lone ranger mentality. The lone ranger mentality is especially easy for those who have been let down depending on other people. While no one likes to be let down, teamwork and collaboration accomplish much more than what can be done alone. Maybe you have some projects, goals, or something else you wish to achieve. While you may be capable of doing it yourself, you can accomplish much more by coming alongside other people who can help you accomplish much more. The adage is true: teamwork makes the dream work. Identify a few people to come alongside you in your efforts, and watch how much farther you will go. Ifeanyi Onuoha sums it up, "Teamwork is the secret that makes common people achieve uncommon results. Alone, we can do so little, but together, we can do so much." Don't do it alone!

Talk to Me God

Can you think of a time when working with others helped you achieve a goal more effectively? How did teamwork enhance the outcome?

What projects or goals do you have right now that could benefit from collaboration? Who can you reach out to for help and support?

The Safe Place

God is our refuge and strength, an ever-present help in trouble.

—Psalm 46:1 (NIV)

My soul finds rest in God alone; my salvation comes from him.

—Psalm 62:1 (NIV)

One night in my home church's family life center, I was sitting in the bleachers waiting for the next basketball game. As I waited, I saw children playing with one another, running around the gym, and chasing each other. I noticed a little girl running from a little boy. She ran all around the gym, but he was still right behind her. It seemed that no matter where she ran, he was right there. The little girl then found the solution—she ran into the girls' restroom. When she ran into the girls' restroom, the little boy stopped at the door because he knew that going behind the door was strictly prohibited. The little girl found safety in the restroom because she knew the little boy would be powerless if she remained in her safe place.

Have you ever felt like the enemy was chasing you? I mean, *really* chasing you? I am talking about being satanically chased at home, at school, at work, in your organization, etc. It seems that no matter what you do, the enemy is right there. When the enemy seems to be in relentless pursuit, you should take refuge in God. It is in God that we find a safe place (room) where we can find rest when we grow weary in the race of life. When you take refuge in God, the enemy

119

must stop at the door because he is fully aware that his ability to penetrate the door of the safe place is strictly prohibited. When the devil is attacking every hand, and weariness is drawing near, run to your safe place in God.

Talk to Me God

How would you establish the habit of taking refuge in God while in difficulty? In what ways could you make God your safe place each day?

Identify one challenge you are facing at the moment and spend some time in prayer, letting God be your refuge by trusting that He will protect and comfort you.

The Blood Bond

Therefore if the Son makes you free, you shall be free indeed.

—John 8:36 (NKJV)

In the city of Memphis, there are many bail bond companies surrounding the local jail. When people are arrested, there is often an option to post bond. To post bond means to put up cash in exchange for freedom. Many people choose this option in order not to spend time in jail, at least immediately. Needless to say, many offenders are thankful for bondsmen who are willing to put up cash for them in order that they may be free.

As people of God, we came into the world spiritually arrested, in bondage to sin. However, there is a Heavenly Bondsman who was willing to post bond for a world of (guilty) sinners. God sent His Son to die in exchange for our freedom. Jesus was the blood bond that was paid for our sins in order that you and I may be free. Once Jesus is accepted as one's personal Savior, Jesus sets you free from the punishment we all deserve. As you look over your life and see where God has brought you from, take a moment to thank God for the blood bond His Son posted for you.

Talk to Me God

Think about how important Jesus' sacrifice was in your freedom from sin. How does this impact your life and your relationship with God on a day-to-day basis?

How can you express gratitude for the freedom that Jesus has given you? What do you have to do or change in order to live life more fully in the freedom He offers?

Celebrate the Days

So, Abraham called that place The LORD Will Provide. And to this day it is said, "On the mountain of the LORD it will be provided.

—Genesis 22:14 (NIV)

[20] And Joshua set up at Gilgal the twelve stones they had taken out of the Jordan. [21] He said to the Israelites, "In the future when your descendants ask their fathers, 'What do these stones mean?' [22] tell them, 'Israel crossed the Jordan on dry ground.'

—Joshua 4:20-22 (NIV)

On September 4, 2000, my Pastor stood before the congregation to announce, "Today, we celebrate the birth of another son in the ministry. Timothy Jackson, Jr. has accepted his call to the ministry." This is a day that I don't think I will ever forget! On this day each year, I reflect on the moment when the ministry God called me to go public. Although ministry has been and continues to be a journey of tremendous highs and lows, I remain honored that God called me. September 4 will always be a special day because it is my exact "birthday," the day I was publicly birthed into ministry.

There are many exact dates and times that stand out in our minds. Some remember the exact day of salvation. Some remember the exact day of baptism. Some remember the exact day healing took place. Some remember the exact day deliverance took place. This list can go on forever! On these exact days, do we take time to reflect and celebrate God for the days? The Israelites set up a memorial to remember

123

crossing the Jordan on dry ground. Abraham named the place where God provided a sacrificial lamb. Many of us celebrate birthdays, retirement, graduation, and other special events. Therefore, let's take time to celebrate God for the 'special events' we have had and continue to have in Him. Celebrate the days!

Talk to Me God

How can you set up reminders or memorials in your life to celebrate and remember God's faithfulness? What are some ways you can celebrate these special moments with others?

Identify a significant spiritual milestone in your life. Take time to reflect on it, thank God for His faithfulness, and find a way to celebrate or commemorate it.

Crazy Jesus

*For God so loved the world that he gave his one and only
Son, that whoever believes in him shall not perish but have
eternal life.*

—John 3:16 (NIV)

*The Word became flesh and made his dwelling among us.
We have seen his glory, the glory of the One and Only, who
came from the Father, full of grace and truth.*

—John 1:14 (NIV)

Imagine that you know a multi-millionaire family. They live
in a multi-million-dollar home with the finest furnishings.
Anything they think of is at their disposal. If they speak a
word, whatever they desire will be given to them. They own
homes throughout the nation, in Florida, California, Colora-
do, New York, and even other parts of the world. They circle
the globe in their travels. Sounds good, doesn't it? Imagine
a member of the family calls you and tells you that he is giving it all up to live in conditions that pale in comparison to
the lifestyle he enjoys. Here is the kicker...The father of the
family didn't lose his job; the money was still plentiful, but he
gave it all up in order to be a blessing to other people. What
would you think of him? Crazy!

This story represents exactly what Jesus did for us. He
left the life of a King to dwell in the projects (you and me).
He left the holiness of Heaven to dwell in and among the
filthy. He left perpetual love to dwell among people who
would hate Him without reason. He left Heaven pleasers to
dwell among hell raisers. Moreover, He left Heaven to die

for people He didn't even know, all of mankind! If we think about how grimy we were (are sometimes), we should appreciate the death, burial, and resurrection of Jesus that much more. From a human perspective, we would consider Jesus crazy to leave Heaven in order to dwell in and among us, but He did, and we should be eternally grateful. Despite all we have done, periodically do, and will do, Jesus was crazy and committed enough to give Himself up for you. Amid all of the craziness of our world, you can securely appreciate the faithfulness of the crazy Jesus who came to save you.

Talk to Me God

How does knowing Jesus left Heaven to live among us deepen your gratitude for His love and sacrifice?

What can you do daily to honor Jesus' sacrifice and show your appreciation?

Spot Me

The LORD himself goes before you and will be with you; he will never leave you nor forsake you. Do not be afraid; do not be discouraged.

—Deuteronomy 31:8 (NIV)

When my father and my mother forsake me, Then the LORD will take care of me.

—Psalm 27:10 (NKJV)

As a former athlete, I believe cheerleaders provide great entertainment at sporting events. While attending a football game at my high school alma mater, two cheerleaders created a pyramid by lifting another young lady high above the ground. While the young lady at the top was being held up, there was always a person behind to spot her. The spotter was there to catch her in case the others around her failed to hold her up. The presence of the spotter made being at the top of the pyramid a little more comfortable because there was someone who would ensure a safe landing to the ground.

Sometimes in life, we find ourselves surrounded by a lot of people. Friends, family, co-workers, classmates, associates, church members, and the list goes on. The people around us craft pyramids of sorts by lavishing us with compliments, gifts, words of encouragement, and other things to lift us up. Obviously, these things are great things to do, and they are certainly enjoyable to receive. But the truth is they are only enjoyable while they last because someone will fail you or has failed you at some point or another. Therefore, there is still the need for the Spotter. Although the people around you

127

mean well, there is always the possibility that they may fail you. The encouragement is that when people fail you, God, the Spotter, is always there to catch you and ensure a safe landing.

Talk to Me God

How will you remember the Lord is always there to catch you when you feel like you're falling? What can you step up to trust Him more with?

Can you think back to a time when you have felt the support of God through a really tough experience? Thank Him for being that Spotter, and share this encouragement with someone who might need it.

It Was Worth It

²Consider it pure joy, my brothers, whenever you face trials of many kinds, ³because you know that the testing of your faith develops perseverance. ⁴Perseverance must finish its work so that you may be mature and complete, not lacking anything.

—James 1:2-4 (NIV)

A scrawny young man decided he wanted to get in shape, so he obtained a gym membership. Because he was fairly skinny, his main desire was to have muscles. He would work out week after week. In many moments, his muscles would be extremely painful. Although the pain was present, he looked forward to the muscles he believed would result from the pain. After a few months of working out and muscular pain, the muscles that he wanted were evident. After considering the progress he made, he declared the pain was worth it.

Lance Armstrong is credited with saying, "Pain is temporary, but quitting lasts forever." It is no secret that life is filled with many painful situations. Painful situations include but are certainly not limited to failing an exam, losing a job, a broken relationship or marriage, the betrayal of a friend or loved one, etc. Being in these circumstances is always tough and painful. Although the pain is there and cannot be ignored, you can look forward to the muscles of faith God will produce because of your current pain. My friend, you will be stronger in the end than you were in the beginning. In the words of Oprah Winfrey, "Turn your wounds into wisdom." Embrace the pain and use it to fuel your future. Someone once said, "Sometimes you have to get knocked down lower than you have ever been to stand back up taller than you ever were." Be assured today that sooner than later, you will look back at the pain and conclude that it was all worth it!

Talk to Me God

How can you remind yourself that current challenges will lead to growth? What can you do to persevere through tough times?

Think of a difficult experience that made you stronger. How did it develop your faith? How can you use this reflection to encourage others?

Just Show Up

[9] *If you declare with your mouth, "Jesus is Lord," and
believe in your heart that God raised him from the dead,
you will be saved.* [10] *For it is with your heart that you
believe and are justified, and it is with your mouth that
you confess and are saved.* [11] *As the Scripture says, "Anyone
who trusts in him will never be put to shame."* [12] *For there
is no difference between Jew and Gentile–the same Lord
is Lord of all and richly blesses all who call on him,* [13] *for,
"Everyone who calls on the name of the Lord will be saved.*

—Romans 10:9-13 (NIV)

Many car dealership commercials saturate the local television programs. No credit checks, trade-in option, cash-back
rebates, and zero percent financing. According to the commercial, the only thing a potential customer must do is show
up. The dealerships are offering "a deal that cannot be refused." Individuals are not required to bring any money to
the table, they do not have to have the best credit, and many
other options are available to the consumer no matter what
condition they are in. The dealership only wants the consumer to simply show up, and they will do the rest.

The greatest commercial that remains in play today is Jesus' commercial for salvation. Jesus' commercial says, "Come
to Me just as you are, and you can gain a relationship with
Me." The past is irrelevant (no credit check). Salvation happens immediately after Jesus is accepted (rebate). Jesus even
offers zero-percent financing, meaning that nothing special
must be done but just show up and speak up by confessing
one's faith in Him! As people of God, we must let the world

know that Jesus is offering them "a deal that cannot or should not be refused." They must know that they cannot get themselves together, the past is irrelevant, and no one is refused. We should let them know that Jesus only wants them to come to Him (show up), speak up (confess), and Jesus will do the rest!

Talk to Me God

How can you remind yourself and others that salvation is available to everyone, no matter their past?

Think of a time when you felt unworthy of God's love. How did showing up and trusting in Him change your perspective?

The Finish Line Is Ahead

[29]He gives strength to the weary and increases the power of the weak. [30]Even youths grow tired and weary, and young men stumble and fall; [31]but those who hope in the LORD will renew their strength. They will soar on wings like eagles; they will run and not grow weary, they will walk and not be faint.

—Isaiah 0:29-31 (NIV)

Reflecting back on my high school basketball days, I thought about what seemed to be the most treacherous pre-season conditioning–running cross-country! Cross-country was a three-mile race to the finish, often through some tough terrain. There were some people who finished the races with ease, though I was certainly not one of them. In fact, it seemed the closer I got to the finish line, the more tired I became. Though I was tired, I would often get a second wind, renewed strength from somewhere within. When I reached the finish line, the joy of simply finishing the race would overcome my weariness.

Oftentimes, we become tired of dealing with things. It seems that the situation(s) continually get worse. It seems that we become wearier as each day goes by. We are running cross-country! The fact that we are becoming tired and weary is a 'tell-tell' sign that the finish line is up ahead. It is the enemy's goal to discourage us and make us stop running because he also knows that the finish line is up ahead. We should be reminded that the darkest hour is just before the break of the day. Today, we must make up our minds that we WILL finish and depend on God to give us a 'second wind' to finish the race! We cannot give up because "the finish line is up ahead!" Hold on!

Talk to Me God

How do you remind yourself that God is with you, giving you strength to finish the race, especially through hard times?

Reflect on a current struggle. Pray for renewed strength to keep moving forward, trusting that the finish line is ahead.

You Can Make It

⁸ We are hard pressed on every side, but not crushed; perplexed, but not in despair; ⁹ persecuted, but not abandoned; struck down, but not destroyed.

—2 Corinthians 4:8-9 (NIV)

In the last devotional, I talked about running cross country as pre-season conditioning for the basketball season. Truthfully, I absolutely hated it! Running around the surrounding neighborhood, climbing the bleachers and stairs, and lifting weights were all a part of the coach's conditioning process and to prepare us for the meets and the season. Often, while running, I felt like I couldn't make it. I would be tired with a capital T and sore with a capital S! However, despite the fatigue and pain, I made it through. When all was said and done, everything I abhorred turned out to be good for me during the season.

There are some times in life when you feel like you just can't make it! Your manager is giving you a tough time, and you feel like you can't make it unless you give him a few choice words. Your children are doing everything *but* what you have asked of them, and you wonder if you can keep your sanity. The challenges and obstacles can seem too large to overcome, leaving you fatigued and in pain. There are many situations that can arise and cause you to question if you can make it. Be encouraged today by knowing that God is with you and has never left your side. You CAN and WILL make it. You cannot afford to be irritated by every rub because if you do, you will never be polished. What you may be experiencing, everything you despise, is just the process

Coach has implemented to prepare you for the season of life you are entering.

Talk to Me God

Recall a time that you experienced overwhelming feelings but got through it. How did God's presence buoy you to keep on moving?

How would you remind yourself that all these challenges are only God's way of preparing you for your future? In what ways might you come to have more trust in His process?

The Wave

If my people, who are called by my name, will humble themselves and pray and seek my face and turn from their wicked ways, then will I hear from heaven and will forgive their sin and will heal their land.

—2 Chronicles 7:14 (NIV)

Let us not give up meeting together, as some are in the habit of doing, but let us encourage one another–and all the more as you see the Day approaching.

—Hebrews 10:25 (NIV)

Yearly, I faithfully attend the annual Southern Heritage Classic Football game hosted in Memphis, TN. Football teams and bands from Historically Black Colleges and Universities (HBCUs) come to the city to compete annually. In the malls and restaurants, you hear alums from each school good-naturedly taunting one another about who will win the game or band competition: At the stadium, fans from each school sit on opposite sides of the stadium, rooting for their respective team or band. At one game, a group of people on one team's side decided to start the wave. After a few short moments, everyone in the stadium participated in the wave. Despite which team attendees were cheering for, everyone in the stadium participated in the same effort—the wave.

People coming together for one common goal and purpose is a tremendous need in our country or world, but especially within the Body of Christ. Race, gender, economic background, political stance, and even ecclesiastical denomination often divide the Body of Christ. The Bible references unity as an important component in the body of Christ. Nevertheless, it is baffling that there are churches on every corner, but the crime rate continually increases. Can you imagine what our world would look like if people joined together to achieve one common goal and purpose? Like the wave, to have people/ministries, irrespective of race, gender, or status, the city and world you live in would be a better place. We talk about how crazy things are in our cities. However, we often fail to put forth the effort to make a change. Former president Barak Obama said, "Be the change you wish to see in the world." Jane Goodall echoes the same sentiment, "What you do makes a difference, and you have to decide what kind of difference you want to make." Maybe *the wave* of change needed in your workplace, community, church, and even the world begins with YOU.

Talk to Me God

How can you contribute to unity and positive change in your community, church, or workplace?

Find something small to do that brings unity and positive change to your community or church; do it today. Start the first step and let others join in.

Look Forward

> [13] *Brothers, I do not consider myself yet to have taken hold of it. But one thing I do: Forgetting what is behind and straining toward what is ahead,* [14] *I press on toward the goal to win the prize for which God has called me heavenward in Christ Jesus.*
>
> —*Philippians 3:13-14 (NIV)*

A young man and his friends were slowly driving along a popular strip in the city where a lot of people hang out. An old, ragged car drove past him on the other side of the street. When the car passed, he began looking in his rear-view mirror to get another look at the car. He was so occupied with the car that he passed by the very people and things he desired to see. Because he was focusing on something behind him, it became impossible for him to see who and what was around him.

Each moment you are given to breathe, you slowly drive down the road of life, hoping to capture the great things or people God has for you. If you are not careful, you can drive past them and miss out because you are too focused on what is behind you. You can overlook new opportunities by fixating on the rear-view mirror of the past. You can miss new chances by constantly looking back at past failures. You can forfeit renewal if you remain focused on the ragged. Don't let your past rob your present or your future. Actor Boris Kodjoe declared, "I can't change history; I don't want to change history. I can only change the future. I'm working on that." You, too, can work on that by choosing to move from the past and intently look forward.

Talk to Me God

How can you remind yourself to focus on the present and future, not the past? How would you implement each of these daily?

How has dwelling on past mistakes or experiences affected your current relationships and opportunities? What can you change in the future to prevent this from happening?

Choose to Speak Life

⁹ With the tongue we praise our Lord and Father, and with it we curse men, who have been made in God's likeness. ¹⁰ Out of the same mouth come praise and cursing. My brothers, this should not be.

—James 3:9-10 (NIV)

Many of us know about playing the dozens. In today's vernacular, playing the dozens is known as roasting or checking. In checking, people negatively talk about one another's clothing, economic status, hairstyle, skin color or condition, job status, family, and so on. What I find amazing is that a person can *check* another person and conclude the *check* by saying, "I'm just playing," as if the statement would eradicate the pain of what was said. If you look at the other friend's face, you will discover that the statement, "I'm just playing," did not expunge the pain and uncomfortable feeling that resulted from the check. The person doing the checking often does not consider the fact that their statements are hurtful, and saying, "I'm just playing," is of no effect in many cases.

Mishandled words can be just as violent as the most dangerous weapons. Paying careful attention to what you say to and about people is imperative. The truth is that believers are frequently guilty of spewing hurtful things, hoping that "I'm just playing" or "I didn't mean any harm" would erase or prevent the hurt. However, there is no return after the statement is made because the wound has been created. "I'm just playing," or a similar statement simply places a band-aid on the wound, but the wound remains. In your everyday dealings, you have opportunities to speak life or death into

141

the lives of those around you. One writer truthfully asserts, "The tongue has no bones, but it is strong enough to break a heart. So be careful with your words." Choose to speak life!

Talk to Me God

What steps can you take to ensure your words build and lift others rather than tear them down? How can you be more aware of the impact of your words?

Today, deliberate on speaking positively to at least three people. Reflect on how your words made some impact.

There is Always Hope

18 While he was saying this, a ruler came and knelt before him and said, "My daughter has just died. But come and put your hand on her, and she will live." 19Jesus got up and went with him, and so did his disciples... 23When Jesus entered the ruler's house and saw the flute players and the noisy crowd, 24he said, "Go away. The girl is not dead but asleep." But they laughed at him. 25After the crowd had been put outside, he went in and took the girl by the hand, and she got up.

—Matthew 9:18-26 (NIV)

In the text above, there is a daughter who everyone in the entire town had given up on and left for dead. Everyone had deemed the girl dead except for one person—her father. The father went to Jesus and asked Him to come to his home and heal his daughter. The people in the town considered the girl to be dead because she had no pulse, could not speak, and had all the characteristics of a dead person. However, when Jesus entered the home, Jesus took the girl's hand and she was raised up. When Jesus stepped into the situation, things changed despite the thoughts and opinions of the people surrounding them.

As with the daughter in the text, many people tend to write others off and count them out based on their present situation. Truthfully, some people may have considered you a hopeless cause at some point. Some said you would never be anything in life. Some counted your marriage or relationship hopeless. Some considered you unqualified to do certain tasks. Some said you would die from your illness. Some said you would be in a certain predicament forever. In fact, even you considered yourself to be hopeless in some ways. However, when Jesus stepped into your life/situation, Jesus made liars out of those who counted you out! You appeared hopeless, but now you are hopeful. People considered you *dead*, but Jesus determined, "This person isn't dead yet," and He made you alive. For those people in your life that frustrate you and cause you to wonder if they will ever be delivered and change, stay prayerful and know He can raise them up just as He raised you up! There is always hope!

Talk to Me God

Reflect on a time when you or someone you know felt hopeless. How did Jesus bring about change? How can this encourage your faith?

How can you offer hope to someone who feels overlooked or defeated? What practical steps can you take to show them that with Jesus, there is always hope?

You Are the Magnet

[15] Neither do people light a lamp and put it under a bowl. Instead, they put it on its stand, and it gives light to everyone in the house. [16] In the same way, let your light shine before men, that they may see your good deeds and praise your Father in heaven.

—*Matthew 5:15-16 (NIV)*

One day, I overhead a conversation between a group of young guys discussing cars. The theme of their conversation was determining what cars could be considered a *chick magnet* car. A chick magnet car is a car that would garner the attention of ladies because they believe that ladies are drawn to nice cars. According to the young men, a chick magnet car has a nice color, leather seats, a great sound system, a sunroof, and anything else that would attract a young lady's attention. All the guys spoke of their desire to drive a *chick magnet* to make themselves more appealing to the ladies.

Have you ever wondered why some people are drawn to you? They only know you for fifteen minutes and share things they have never shared with anyone else. You are the person they seek advice from. It seems you are the only person they talk to at work, school, or some other place. Sometimes, you sit and wonder, "Why are they coming to me when they don't even know me?" Here it is…You are the magnet! To the young men above, women are drawn to a car based mainly on outward appearances. People come to you because they can see the presence of God in your life. They observe how you handle difficult situations and notice the peace of God in your life. They sense the godly love in your interactions with others and see the love of God in your eyes when you speak. Know that you are a magnet, and that is precisely what God desires you to be! As one writer says, "Live in such a way that those who know you but don't know God will come to know God because they know you." People are attracted to the light you emit, not because of your perfection but because of your authenticity. The next time you wonder why someone is opening up to you, just know you are a magnet for God to draw people closer to Him.

Talk to Me God

In what ways do you think your relationship with God influences how others perceive and interact with you?

Have you recently experienced a moment when someone was unexpectedly drawn to you or sought your advice? How did you respond, and what did it reveal about your impact on their life?

The Spirit Has Your Back

25 But if we hope for what we do not yet have, we wait for it patiently. 26 In the same way, the Spirit helps us in our weakness. We do not know what we ought to pray for, but the Spirit himself intercedes for us with groans that words cannot express.

—*Romans 8:26 (NIV)*

I often reflect on my childhood and how blessed I was. To this day, I remain amazed at how it seemed that my late mother always knew what I needed or even wanted without my asking. If I needed a word of encouragement, she would say exactly what I needed to hear without my saying anything. When I needed money in college, I would receive an unexpected yet timely check in the mail. It appeared that my mother knew my every thought, which was and remains amazing to me. I would often wonder, "How did she know what I needed and wanted?" Because I wanted to eliminate any measure of worry about me and be self-sufficient as a college student, I often didn't know how to ask. Though I didn't know how to ask, somehow Mae Ree Jackson seemed to hear my plea.

Have you ever been at a point in your life where you needed God for something, but didn't know how or what to say? You were in so much pain that when you fell to your knees in prayer, you couldn't gather the words to say. Your heart and mind said, "I need to talk to God about this," however, the words could not find their way out of your mouth. Be reminded of today's Scripture that God is the ultimate Parent and knows what you need before you ask Him. Know that God knows YOUR situation. God knows YOUR concerns.

He understands that sometimes pain overwhelms you and you are too weak to say anything. Be thankful today that God understands your prayers even when the words are missing. In the times when you can't find the words to say and the strength to say it, know that the Holy Spirit is interceding on your behalf.

Talk to Me God

Have you ever experienced a moment where you struggled to find the right words in prayer but felt a sense of comfort or support anyway? How did that experience strengthen your faith?

In what areas of your life are you currently waiting for something you hope for? How does knowing that the Holy Spirit intercedes on your behalf help you in your journey of patience and trust?

Trust the Manager's Measurements

*For I know the plans I have for you," declares the LORD,
"plans to prosper you and not to harm you, plans to give
you hope and a future.*

—*Jeremiah 29:11 (NIV)*

As the best man in my friend's wedding, it was necessary that I
get fitted for the tuxedo that would be worn for the wedding.
I went to a local tuxedo shop and the manager used a measuring tape to acquire my measurements. Interestingly, the
measurements she obtained were a bit different from what
I was accustomed to. As I told her the measurements I was
accustomed to, she explained in a rather sarcastic manner
that she has the measuring tape and knows how the tuxedo
is supposed to fit. Though I wanted to snap back, I immediately realized that as the manager, she knew what was best.
The day before the wedding, I went to try on the tuxedo, it fit
perfectly. The tuxedo fit perfectly only because I trusted the
manager's measurements in lieu of my own.

Let's be honest, you know what you like and don't like.
You know what you want and what you don't want. You know
yourself better than anyone else, right? After all, you have
been living and knowing you for a long time. Therefore, you
have come to know your measurements. Not! There is Someone who knows you better than you know you. However, you
can become so accustomed to doing things a certain way
and desiring everything to fit your way of doing things, your
measurements. The stark reality is that God's measurements

for your life can be much different from your own and if we are honest, it can be difficult to take God's word for it. My friend, God understands you more deeply than you understand yourself. God sees you more clearly than you see yourself. God knows your heart better than you do. In fact, God is more familiar with your true self than you are. As the Divine Manager of your life, trust God and His experience to capture the perfect fit for your life. Admittedly, it can be tough to trust God's measurements for your life when you don't understand what God is doing. Just remember God is the manager and has been in business since the beginning of time. When you face situations that make no sense to you, trust the Manager's measurements.

Talk to Me God

In what areas do you struggle to trust God's plans over your own? How could surrendering to God's guidance shift your perspective or outcomes?

Reflect on a time you were uncertain about trusting God's direction. How did it turn out, and what did you learn about relying on His wisdom instead of your own?

No Second Opinion Needed

Jesus replied, "I tell you the truth, if you have faith and do not doubt, not only can you do what was done to the fig tree, but also you can say to this mountain, 'Go, throw yourself into the sea,' and it will be done.

—Matthew 21:21 (NIV)

When a person goes to the doctor and receives a certain diagnosis, it is often suggested they gain a second opinion. Though the primary doctor may suggest surgery or some other invasive measure, it is considered a good idea to get a second opinion. By obtaining a second opinion, that person can better determine if his or her primary doctor and another doctor have a consensus concerning the diagnosis.

Has God ever spoken something to you, and you sought a second opinion from someone else? You can receive divine instructions yet seek human approval. What did God tell you? Did God tell you to go for the house, but the second opinion told you that you shouldn't? Did God tell you to apply or try out, but the second opinion said you were unqualified or incapable? Here is the question of the day for you...Whose opinion matters? You would rather have God's approval above and beyond man's applause. Grace Wesley takes it a step further; you would rather stand with God and be judged by the world than stand with the world and be judged by God. When God speaks into your life, His opinion is the only *truth* that matters; no second opinion is needed. Too many people value the opinions of mothers, fathers, sisters, brothers, friends, and pastors. Although one values one's opinions concerning certain issues, God's opinion should be second to none. As one gospel song states, "Just because God said it, that's enough for me." There may be something God is leading you to do that others or even your family may not agree with; remember God said it, and no second opinion is needed.

Talk to Me God

Have you ever hesitated to follow God's direction due to others' opinions? How might trusting Him without seeking a second opinion have changed the outcome?

Reflect on a time when you followed God's lead despite contrary advice. How did this strengthen your faith in His plan for you?

It's In the Lord's Hands

¹⁴But I trust in you, O LORD; I say, "You are my God." ¹⁵
My times are in your hands; deliver me from my enemies
and from those who pursue me. ¹⁶ *Let your face shine on*
your servant; save me in your unfailing love.

—*Psalm 31:14-16 (NIV)*

Years ago, I received an e-mail entitled "Depends on Whose
Hands It's In," that compared the value of certain items
based on whose hands the items were in. It talked about how
a basketball in my hands would be worth about $20, but a
basketball in Michael Jordan's hands is worth millions. A golf
ball in my hands is worth a few dollars, but worth millions in
the hands of Tiger Woods. A baseball in my hands is worth
minimal dollars, but worth millions in the hands of Barry
Bonds. The value of the items depends on whose hands they
are in.

Contrary to popular belief, the Christian comprises both
good and bad times. There are times when you are happy,
and times you are not so happy. You have periods when it
seems everything is going right and times when it seems everything is going wrong. There are times you feel well and
times when you don't. There are times of love and times of
persecution. Times may vary month to month, week to week,
day to day, hour by hour, or even moment by moment. However, no matter what state you find yourself in, your current
times are in the Lord's hands. Your happy times are in the
Lord's hands. Difficult times are in the Lord's hands. Mel-
ancholy times are in the Lord's hands. Sometimes, you need
to be reminded that ALL your life's circumstances and times

Talk to Me God Devotionals Volume 2

are under God's control. Don't lose your faith. The legendary Dr. Gardner Taylor said, "Faith is the capacity of the soul to perceive the unseen. It is the spiritual organ of perception. At this very moment in your life, whatever time it is, don't be discouraged, but remember that your times are in the Lord's Hands. Things will always be better when they are in the Lord's Hands.

Talk to Me God

How does the idea that all your life's circumstances are under God's control change how you approach your successes and struggles?

Think of a time when you found it hard to believe God controlled your situation. What steps can you take to trust in God's guidance during similar situations in the future?

It Will Come To Past

The one who calls you is faithful and he WILL do it."

—1 Thessalonians 5:24 (NIV)

But those who wait on the LORD; Shall renew their strength; They shall mount up with wings like eagles, They shall run and not be weary, They shall walk and not faint.

—Isaiah 40:31 (KJV)

Have you ever been in the drive-thru of a fast-food restaurant and it seemed like an eternity to get your food? You place your order and after a while, you notice that you haven't moved much from that point in the line. You are tired, have somewhere to go, and are hungry, and other factors frustrate you as you wait to get your food. A part of you is tempted to get out of line and go home or go some other place. However, leaving would cause you to forfeit the opportunity to satisfy your hunger. Although you are frustrated, you continue to wait because you know that, at some point, you will eventually reach the window and receive what you have been waiting for.

Is there something you have asked of God and it seems God is taking an eternity to come to pass? You have prayed, fasted, made your request, and even received confirmation that Heaven heard your request. Even so, weeks, months, or possibly years, and you haven't moved much. You find yourself tired and frustrated, and begin to question if God has forgotten about you. You want God to hurry with your requests. In a real sense, you desire a *fast-food* blessing. Rev. Charles Blake encourages you with these words, "in your waiting,

God does some of His best work. Don't rush the process." As with waiting in a drive-thru, no matter how hungry you are for it or how frustrated you become, the unfortunate truth is that you still must wait. You must be in a place where you can accept temporary disappointment yet hold on to your hope. You may be tempted to get out of line by giving up, but that would cause you to forfeit your blessing. However, the blessing of waiting is knowing that you will eventually reach the *window*. Dr. Gina Stewart says it best, "God's timing may not align with our expectations, but His timing is always perfect. Be still and know He is at work."

Talk to Me God

What is a current situation in your life where you feel you are waiting indefinitely for God's answer? How can you stay encouraged and trust that God's timing is perfect?

How can you shift your perspective from seeing waiting as a frustrating delay to recognizing it as an opportunity for growth and preparation in your spiritual journey?

Hand It Over

> [6] *Therefore humble yourselves under the mighty hand of God, that He may exalt you in due time,* [7] *casting all your care upon Him, for He cares for you.*
>
> —*1 Peter 5:6-7 (NIV)*

As I was leaving the building, I noticed a young lady carrying a heavy box to her car. When I offered to carry the box for her, she refused. I was nearly offended because I felt it was my responsibility to carry the heavy load for her, whether she knew me or not. I was also wondering what people in the vicinity were thinking about me as a man as I walked beside a young lady carrying this heavy load, and my hands were empty. The young lady was so intent on being independent that she refused to allow me to carry what was obviously too heavy. As I continued to walk beside her (semi-upset), watching her struggle to her car, my mind was screaming, "I wish this woman would just hand it over!"

Though the story above is somewhat humorous, you may be more analogous to the young lady than you think. How? I am glad you asked. The fact is that we often carry things that God has offered to carry for us. What are examples of 'heavy loads' we carry? "How am I going to do it?" "Is the situation ever going to change?" "Will I ever find a job?" "Will I be able to handle it?" You get the picture; just add your *heavy load* statement to the list. Truthfully speaking, countless but futile hours can be spent being independent and figuring things out for yourself. In a real sense, this is altogether pointless. We have God who is willing and able to carry the heavy loads for us. Maybe you are worried about something you can do absolutely nothing about. Picture God walking beside you offended because you proclaim to trust Him but refuse to hand over what concerns us. Today, God is screaming to you from Heaven saying, "I wish my son and daughter would just hand it over!"

Talk to Me God

What are some heavy burdens or worries you currently carry that you need to hand to God? How can you begin to trust Him more fully with these concerns?

In what ways might your desire for independence be causing you to struggle unnecessarily? How can you learn to let go and allow God to carry those burdens for you?

Pre-Registration Only

*Jesus answered, "I am the way and the truth and the life.
No one comes to the Father except through me.*

—John 14:6 (NIV)

When attending a conference or workshop, pre-registration is almost always encouraged. In pre-registration, you submit the necessary information and associated fees so your name is on file at the door. While some conferences and workshops offer onsite registration, others have a pre-registration-only policy that is firmly implemented. Despite how much a person may desire to attend, no matter how much they beg or plead, regardless of how much they offer to pay, the policy is pre-registration only.

As we look at today's society, many people live their lives as if God offers onsite registration at the gate of Heaven. Some seem to assume they have plenty of time to *get it together* and align their lives with God. Some say they will ask for forgiveness and give their lives to Christ *when the time is right.* The list can go on and on about the many excuses people use to live how they want. Whatever the case, to attend Heaven's eternal conference of believers, God's policy is pre-registration only. The time is now! No one (and I mean no one) has the power to get themselves together. If anyone had the power to get themselves together, they would have done it already. Tomorrow or even the next 3 minutes are not promised to anyone. God doesn't ask for money. He wants a made-up mind. God doesn't ask for a completed form but He wants complete faith. Believers must encourage unsaved loved ones and friends to get saved because Heaven is for those who are pre-registered by accepting Him as Lord and Savior.

Talk to Me God

In what areas of your life are you delaying your commitment to God, thinking you have more time? What steps can you take today to ensure your heart fully aligns with Him?

How can you actively share the message of "pre-registration" for Heaven with your loved ones and friends? What actions can you take to encourage them to accept Jesus as their Savior?

It Ain't Over

³But you are a shield around me, O LORD; you bestow glory on me and lift up my head. ⁴ To the LORD I cry aloud, and he answers me from his holy hill.

—Psalm 3:3-4 (NIV)

Years ago, I witnessed the Indianapolis Colts defeat the Tampa Bay Buccaneers during a Monday night football game. The Colts were down by three touchdowns with only minutes left in the game. Many people turned their televisions off or went to another station, believing the game was out of reach and that the Buccaneers would win. However, although many counted the Colts out, they came back and won the game in the last few minutes! Although people had given up on them, they didn't give up on themselves and ultimately won the game that many thought they would lose. Until the last second of the game, the Colts maintained an "it ain't over" mind frame.

There may be a situation in your life you feel is in the last few minutes. It looks like things will not get better. It looks like someone else is going to get it. It seems that time is running out. It looks like it's not going to work out. You may have people around you "prophesying" that it can't or won't happen, giving you a list of unsolicited reasons why they believe it's out of reach. The truth is, you don't need anyone adding to the doubt you're already struggling with. Even you are beginning to wonder if what you desire is out of reach. My friend, as long as breath is in your body and God remains on the throne, there is still time in the game, and the great Coach is still on your sideline. Despite how things may appear, IF you don't give up on God or yourself, you will achieve what many (even you) thought you would lose. It ain't over!

Talk to Me God

Reflect on a seemingly hopeless situation in your life. How can you remind yourself that "it ain't over" and keep your faith strong?

Have you experienced a last-minute turnaround? How did it shape your faith and perseverance?

It's Not within Walking Distance

In the same way, faith by itself, if it is not accompanied by action, is dead.

—*James 2:17 (NIV)*

While in college, the basic things I needed were available in places that were within walking distance. Snacks, laundry detergent, and small restaurants could all be found in a nearby mini-mart. However, when I wanted to step it up a bit, those places were not within walking distance. The nice restaurants, music stores, and shopping malls required a longer trip. Therefore, in order to get to the greater places, I had to put forth extra effort to get to them. Lacking a car, I often found the task challenging, but when I got there, it was well worth the effort.

As Christians, we often want things to come easily. The reality is that nothing worth having will come easy. I imagine many things you would like to see, do, or be done. In reality, the desire is many times greater than the effort. Many people are guilty of the fact that sometimes they fail to put forth the effort necessary to accomplish the very things they say they desire. You can want the prize but not be willing to embrace the process to get it. In a real sense, you want what you want to be within walking distance, not requiring much effort. The reality is that thoughts and ideas are no good without action. When we think of what it takes to pursue our dreams, we give up because we want things to be within walking distance. Vidal Sassoon said that "the only place where success comes before work is in the dictionary." Although extra effort is required, know there are greater things in store for you in places/situations that may not be within walking distance. It is your time to act on what you have thought about for weeks, months, maybe years! That which you dream of will come to pass only when action is put forth, all while realizing it's not within walking distance.

Talk to Me God

What dreams or goals have you hesitated to pursue because they require extra effort? What steps can you take today to move closer to them?

How can you remind yourself to combine faith with action, especially when the journey seems long and challenging?

Don't Hold Back

¹ I will extol the LORD at all times; his praise will always be on my lips. ² My soul will boast in the LORD; let the afflicted hear and rejoice.

—Psalm 34:1-2 (NIV)

Imagine this...You are seventeen years old and talked to your parents about an item you really want. It could be a car, outfit, television, money, or anything else you REALLY desire! Imagine you come home and the thing you wanted was parked in the driveway, lying on your bed, or just dropped in your hand. How would you respond? I can see you now! I see you jumping, shouting excitedly, dancing, and excessively hugging and kissing the person who gave it to you. Your appreciation and excitement at the moment are too great to be contained. Am I right about it? Absolutely, I am! ☺

As you imagine the scenario above, assess how you respond to God when God does amazing things for you. Just think about it. The fact you are reading this devotional with your eyes and fingers is a testament to the keeping power of God. In the book *God is Able*, Priscilla Shirer says, "we have no idea of the activity God is currently orchestrating in our lives. You have been spared some tragedies, you have been shielded from certain evils, you have been steered clear of dangerous people and situations that could have done you in. God may have healed you from sickness you didn't even know you were ill with. He may have rectified circumstances on your behalf before your knowledge or awareness of an issue." These are the things God is doing behind the scenes in your life, but there are a number of things God has done and

165

is doing for you with an open curtain. There are many things you REALLY desire that God has given you. The question of the day is how you responded and how you are responding to God honoring your request. Give God the thanks or praise God deserves. As you think about the many things God has done for you and who God is, praise Him accordingly. One author states it this way, "if you can think, you can thank (Him). If you can thank (Him), you can praise (Him)." Don't hold back!

Talk to Me God

How do you express gratitude to God for His blessings and protection? What steps can you take to ensure you don't hold back your praise?

Can you recall a time when God answered your prayers in an extraordinary way? How did you respond, and how can you share that testimony to encourage others' faith?

Red Light, Green Light

...Today, if you hear his voice, do not harden your hearts.

—Hebrews 4:7 (NIV)

As a child, I remember playing a game called, "Red Light, Green Light." In this game, all participants begin at the same point on the playground while the director stands at the finish line. When the director yelled, 'green light,' we would all run in an attempt to reach the finish line. As we ran, the director would then scream, 'Red light,' and each person attempted to stop in their tracks. If someone lost their balance or continued to run after the director said 'red light,' they were considered to be out of the game. In short, the key to the game was to listen closely to the director as each of us attempted to be the first to reach the finish line. However, it was vital not to run too fast.

Life in the Kingdom of God is likened to a game of "Red Light, Green Light." As you run the Christian race, you must stay in tune with the Director. When God says 'green light,' run and do what He asks you to do. However, no matter how badly you may aspire to reach a certain point, it is vital that you are able to stop when God speaks 'red light.' Wanting things in *your* time, when *you* want them, where *you* want them, and how *you* want them causes you to be off-balance, continuing to run when you should stop. This can result in your forfeiting the very things God longs to do with and for you. Being off balance and running when we shouldn't will almost always cause a loss of some kind. As you strive to reach the finish line, the destiny God has for your life, listen closely to the Director, and by all means, don't run too fast.

Talk to Me God

Are you attuned to God's signals, knowing when to move and when to pause? How can you better discern His voice?

Reflect on a time when not waiting for God's timing led to a missed opportunity. What did you learn from that experience?

It's Just a Pop-Up

³For though we walk in the flesh, we do not war according to the flesh. ⁴For the weapons of our warfare are not carnal but mighty in God for pulling down strongholds, ⁵casting down arguments and every high thing that exalts itself against the knowledge of God, bringing every thought into captivity to the obedience of Christ.

—2 Corinthians 10:3-5 (NKJV)

Before the invention of pop-up blockers, I would frequently get irritated by the constant pop-ups interrupting me as I tried to search for things. I almost felt like the pop-up concept was created to be an irritant. When I opened the page I wanted, a pop-up would come up. As I browsed a site, pop-ups would surface again and again. Every time a pop-up came up, I didn't even read it, but I closed it out quickly because my focus was on what I was trying to accomplish.

Time and again, when you are focused on God and the things of God, the enemy consistently sends pop-ups your way in an effort to distract you from your goal or purpose. What is a pop-up? Here it is...You are in a good mood, and someone says something out of line that upsets you—that's a pop-up. You are blessed with some extra money, and something happens that requires you to spend it, something you had no plans to purchase or repair—that's a pop-up. You are driving along the streets of your city, fully engaged in your personal praise fest, and someone cuts you off—that's a pop-up. In short, pop-ups are anything sent to distract you from focusing on God and the things God would have you do. TD Jakes echoes, "The enemy's tactic is distraction. If he can keep your focus off God, he can keep you from your destiny." When pop-ups come up in your life, do not get upset and distracted, but quickly close them out so you can focus on what God is saying and calling you to.

Talk to Me God

What "pop-ups" have recently distracted you from focusing on God?

How can you better recognize and dismiss these distractions to align with your spiritual goals?

Call Technical Support

¹ I lift up my eyes to the hills, where does my help come from?
² My help comes from the LORD, the Maker of heaven and
earth. ³ He will not let your foot slip-he who watches over
you will not slumber; ⁴ indeed, he who watches over Israel
will neither slumber nor sleep.

—Psalm 121:1-4 (NIV)

One night, a man was experiencing issues with his home computer. He tried various things to resolve the issues, but nothing seemed to work. He ensured all the connections were properly in place, but that was to no avail. After a great deal of frustration and an hour of trying to figure things out, he finally decided to contact the 24-hour technical support center for assistance. Interestingly, technical support was able to fix the problem almost immediately. The man began on all the time he wasted because he didn't seek technical support in the beginning.

Living in a smart world, we regularly find ourselves attempting to handle issues and problems on our own. You try this and that, but nothing seems to work. After a while, you find yourself frustrated because it has been hours, weeks, months, or years, and little to no progress has been made. Your God is the ultimate Technical Support person who is always available for assistance. God is available 24/7 and is more than capable to immediately fix what you cannot. If and when you call on divine Technical Support, God will reveal to you all the time you wasted because you neglected to call on Him in the beginning. Whatever the issues or problems in life, don't try to figure things out; call on the Lord for assistance. Let's sum it up in the words of Joyce Meyer, "The more you try to handle things on your own, the more you realize how much you need God's help."

Talk to Me God

What challenges have you been trying to handle on your own?

How can you remind yourself to seek God's help first instead of waiting until you're frustrated?

Locked Up

¹³ Moses answered the people, "Do not be afraid. Stand firm and you will see the deliverance the LORD will bring you today. The Egyptians you see today you will never see again. ¹⁴ The LORD will fight for you; you need only to be still.

—*Exodus 14:13-14 (NIV)*

As a child, my father and I would sometimes sit and watch movies together. In one movie, a man was in jail, talking and behaving uncontrollably. After a while of dealing with the man, the officers put him in a straitjacket and a muzzle-like apparatus over his mouth. While in the straitjacket, the man was locked into one position. Although he wanted to move, he was unable to. With the muzzle over his mouth, you could see that he wanted to talk but was unable to. The man was locked in where the officers needed him to be so they could do what they needed to do for the man.

When certain things happen in our lives, you can feel like you are going crazy! You know what I mean? It seems that people continually offend you; the more you love people, and the more they let you down, the more you try to emerge from the mountain of debt, the more things happen to prevent you from doing so. If you are not careful, you can allow emotions to gain the upper hand, leading you to say or do something God disapproves of. Rather, it is in these moments that God desires to place us in a metaphorical straitjacket and muzzle. Characteristics of being in God's straitjacket are when all the options have been exhausted, such as when you want to move but lack direction, a destination, and whatever

173

Talk to Me God Devotionals Volume 2

else you wish to add. Characteristics of sporting God's muzzle are when you have complained, grumbled, and cried all you could, your well of words is now empty except for a few choice words reserved for a particular person or two, and whatever else you wish to add. When life lands you in a place where you have no more moves and you lack the words to say, you are exactly where God needs you to be for Him to do what needs to be done in you and for you.

Talk to Me God

When have you felt locked in place by life's challenges, unable to move or speak freely?

How can you practice being still and trusting God to fight for you during challenging times?

Try a New Move

See, I am doing a new thing! Now it springs up; do you not perceive it? I am making a way in the wilderness and streams in the wasteland.

—*Isaiah 43:19 (NIV)*

In the early days of the internet and computers, Solitaire was one of my favorite computer games. During study or work breaks, I would often spend my time playing it. One of the first things I realized about Solitaire was that it took a different approach to win each game. The same approach that worked in one game would not work in another game. Although it was the same game of Solitaire, it took a different approach to accomplish the same goal. If the same approach worked, I would likely have become bored with it and stopped playing it altogether. In order for me to continue enjoying the game, I had to be open to new moves.

Because we are creatures of habit, it is easy to become routine in how we do things day to day and how we handle certain situations. You can become accustomed to doing things a certain way and have found a measure of success in doing things exactly that way. Even so, there are times that you discover that the same method is not as efficient. "This is the way I have always done it,' 'I've always been like this,' 'It worked last time,' 'I got it last time,' 'This is what they did and it worked, so what's wrong now?" These are a few statements that come to mind when old methods do not produce new results breeding frustration and disappointment. During these times, you must remain open to new directions and actions that God may be leading you to take to achieve the same goal. If God allows you to become routine, you could likely become bored with it, thereby attempting to predict God's future movement and activity in your life. You may be frustrated at this point in life because what you have always done or said is proving impotent; take a moment to pray and ask God to show you a new move.

Talk to Me God

In what areas of your life have you been relying on old methods that are no longer working, and how has this caused frustration or disappointment?

How can you intentionally remain open to new directions and guidance from God, especially when you feel stuck or when old methods are ineffective?

Bingo

.

Shouts of joy and victory resound in the tents of the righteous: "The LORD's right hand has done mighty things!

—Psalm 118:15 (NIV)

As it is written: "I have made you a father of many nations." He is our father in the sight of God, in whom he believed–the God who gives life to the dead and calls things that are not as though they were.

—Romans 4:17 (NIV)

Before the days of dog races and casinos became popular, Bingo was the game to play. Many older citizens in the community would routinely go to local centers along with their friends to play Bingo. In the game of Bingo, each person is given a card (or several cards depending on skill level) with numbers corresponding with the letters B.I.N.G.O along with a set of chips. The chips were to serve as markers. When each letter and number were called, one would place a chip on the respective card. When the necessary spaces were covered, that person would yell "Bingo" to notify everyone of their victory. Here is the thing: a person could have all the spaces covered, but if they failed to speak out "Bingo," their victory would be null and void. On the other hand, there were moments when people would get excited and yell "Bingo" when all their spaces weren't covered. They shouted "Bingo" prematurely in anticipation of a victory they looked to experience.

There have been a multitude of spaces in your life you needed God to cover and step into. You've needed His presence in situations at work or school, at home, in relationships, in your children's lives, and in countless other areas. By God's grace, God covered the spaces in your life you needed Him to fill and gave you victory. Unfortunately, and to God's dismay, we can sometimes sit with our spaces covered and not shout to God as a thank you, for God has allowed victory. Do you thank God for the things He has done? I mean, really thank God for the things God has done? If God delivered you from anything–Bingo! If God delivered you from toxic relationships and friendships–Bingo! God provided what you did not deserve or could not afford—Bingo! God opened a door you were not qualified for—Bingo! You passed the exam that paved the way for your graduation or career—Bingo! At this very moment, you have something to thank God for. In fact, you can shout thanks to God in anticipation of the victory you are looking to experience in the spaces God has not yet covered. A.W Tozer encapsulates it, "Gratitude is an offering precious in the sight of God, and it is one that the poorest of us can make and be not poorer but richer for having made it."

Talk to Me God

How often do you take the time to genuinely thank God for the victories and blessings He has brought into your life, and how can you make this a regular practice?

What are the areas in your life where you need God to step in and cover the spaces, and how can you express your faith and gratitude in anticipation of His help?

The Key Component

But seek first his kingdom and his righteousness, and all these things will be given to you as well.

—*Matthew 6:33 (NIV)*

Before the days of social media and text messages, e-mail was the best way to communicate with multiple people simultaneously. As an associate minister who did not preach on a regular basis, people would often ask me to let them know when I would minister. When I was privileged with an assignment, I would send an e-mail inviting family and friends to worship. On one occasion, I sent an e-mail invitation but neglected to include the time. I included everything in the e-mail except the time! Obviously, the time was a key component in the e-mail. The service could have been at any time. In the eyes of someone who wished to come, my initial e-mail was useless without the time being noted. It was missing the key component. An e-mail without the time is like Kool-Aid without sugar, ham without a burger, or macaroni without cheese! The key component was necessary for the e-mail to be complete.

Have you ever realized you were missing a key component? Maybe you went to the grocery store and left your money at home, went to the mall to make a return and forgot the receipt, or went to work and left your ID behind? There are seasons and moments when you have everything else but still lack the key component. The key component for the believer is prayer. Dr. Tony Evans describes prayer as the key to connecting us to God's heart. The greatest danger for the believer is to navigate the labyrinth of life without prayer. Dr.

EV Hill says, "Not praying is like driving without a map. You may keep moving, but you'll be lost and without direction. Prayer keeps us on God's path." Missing the key component of prayer can land you in toxic, unhealthy situations and relationships. Missing the key component of prayer can cause you to accept a job because of pay and benefits, but it is in the margins of God's will. There is not enough time or space in this book to list the pitfalls we can experience when we fail to pray. Take this moment to pray and seek God FIRST about whatever is before you, for that is the key component.

Talk to Me God

In what areas of your life have you neglected the critical component of prayer, and how can you prioritize seeking God first in these areas?

Reflect on a time when missing the critical component of prayer led to confusion or difficulty. How can this experience remind you to always include prayer in your decision-making process?

Housekeeping

Here I am! I stand at the door and knock. If anyone hears my voice and opens the door, I will come in and eat with him, and he with me. [21] *To him who overcomes, I will give the right to sit with me on my throne, just as I overcame and sat down with my Father on His throne.*

—*Revelation 3:20-21 (NIV)*

The housekeeping team at my workplace has a policy when it comes to cleaning restrooms in the building. The policy is to "knock before entering." When the housekeeper comes to each restroom, they knock on the door, say "housekeeping," and then wait for a response from someone who may be in the restroom. If someone is in the restroom, they stand outside and will not enter until they are given permission. After receiving permission, the housekeeper goes in and cleans.

God is our heavenly Housekeeper who, from the beginning of time, implemented a "knock before entering" policy for our lives. Although God can do whatever God wishes, there are some things God will not do without your permission. In fact, God doesn't even enter our lives without our consent. If God does not enter our lives forcibly, God will certainly not enter some circumstances until given permission. Frequently, we attempt to deal with things on our own and find that our efforts are worthless. While we struggle and continuously come up short, God stands outside the situation, saying, "housekeeping," waiting for permission to come in and clean things up. Standing on the outside, God possesses all the supplies needed for any situation. All He needs is permission to enter. Give God permission today. In the words of one of my favorite people, the late Pastor Laurence O. Hudson, "A prayer that is not prayed is a prayer that won't be answered."

Talk to Me God

What areas of your life have you been trying to handle independently without inviting God in? How can you give God permission to intervene and clean things up?

Reflect on a time when you permitted God to enter a situation in your life. How did His involvement change the outcome? How can this experience encourage you to seek His help more readily?

Don't Quit

Let us not become weary in doing good, for at the proper time we will reap a harvest if we do not give up.

—Galatians 6:9 (NIV)

...The race is not to the swift or the battle to the strong, nor does food come to the wise or wealth to the brilliant or favor to the learned; but time and chance happen to them all.

—Ecclesiastes 9:11 (NIV)

Trying to hone skills learned in the Chess Club at school, my twin children were playing chess one Saturday afternoon. Throughout the game, she becomes frustrated because it appears her brother is defeating her. During their game, my daughter Avery had a straight shot to conquer her brother's king, who was the object of the game. Though she had the perfect break to take, she stopped in one space before taking his king. She had an opportunity to win but forfeited the victory simply because she quit too soon. The goal was at her fingertips, but because she became frustrated, she stopped too soon.

It is no secret that life is filled with moments of frustration, confusion, and dismay. As one pursues a goal, it seems as if every possible obstacle or challenge seems to arrive at the doorstep of your life at the most opportune times. Financial challenges, emotional despair, and relational issues, among many other things, can cause frustration to take over. If we are not careful, that frustration can cloud our judgment to the degree that the goal can be at our fingertips but be forfeited because we quit. Former First Lady Michelle Obama once said, "You should never view your challenges as a disadvantage. Instead, it's important for you to understand that your experience facing and overcoming adversity is actually one of your biggest advantages." Whatever challenges or obstacles you are facing in pursuit of your goal, keep going and do not quit until victory is achieved!

Talk to Me God

What is causing you frustration, confusion, and dismay in your current pursuits? How can you shift your perspective to see these challenges as opportunities for growth?

Are there areas in your life where you have felt like quitting? How can you ask God for the strength and perseverance to stay in the race and see it through to victory?

Your Father Is Looking Out for You

¹ *Whoever dwells in the shelter of the Most High*
  will rest in the shadow of the Almighty.
² *I will say of the Lord, "He is my refuge and my fortress,*
  my God, in whom I trust."
³ *Surely he will save you*
  from the fowler's snare
  and from the deadly pestilence.
⁴ *He will cover you with his feathers,*
  and under his wings you will find refuge;
  his faithfulness will be your shield and rampart.

  —Psalm 91:1-4 (NIV)

One year, while celebrating the Fourth of July, several kids were at the family home popping fireworks. It seemed the sparklers were the favorite of the smaller kids. Of course, when children are excited, they move aimlessly without much regard for other people. At one moment, a kid was flailing a burning sparkler as he walked around in pure fascination. As he walked around, fascinated by the sparkler, he came near my son, who was not paying any attention and was in the path of the burning sparkler. Seeing what my son did not see, I simply moved him out of the way to prevent him from being burned. My son was completely oblivious to the danger his father protected him from while he enjoyed life as only a kid knows how.

As people of God, we are often oblivious to the many dangers that surround us moment by moment. Dangers ranging from natural disasters to people's attacks are always present in all our lives. There is great comfort in knowing that although dangers are all around us, God is divinely orchestrating things in both the natural and spiritual world that protect us even when we are unaware. The saints of antiquity were right in thanking God for protecting us from dangers seen and unseen. Even now, as you read this devotional, God is protecting you from something you are completely unaware of. God is looking out for you!

Talk to Me God

What are some things you are certain God protected you from?

Take a moment to thank God for the things noted and what you are unaware of.

Do Not Force It

[8] *"For my thoughts are not your thoughts, neither are your ways my ways," declares the Lord.*

[9] *"As the heavens are higher than the earth, so are my ways higher than your ways and my thoughts than your thoughts.*

—*Isaiah 55:8-9 (NIV)*

While preparing a sermon in my home office, my twin children joined attempting to assemble a puzzle on the floor. At one point, they began trying to force two pieces together, causing them frustration. I looked at the pieces and immediately determined that they were becoming frustrated with something that simply did not fit to create the picture they were striving for. I said, "Twins, the pieces y'all have don't go together. Y'all are trying to force them." They replied, "But Daddy, they do go together," and continued trying to force them to fit. I decided not to debate with them; I just sat back in my chair and watched them. After a few moments, they soon realized their father was right and accepted the fact they were trying to force what did not fit.

Have you been guilty of trying to force people or things into your life that simply do not fit? Oftentimes, the opportunity looks perfect and certainly checks all the boxes in your mind, but somehow it just does not seem to work. That person seems perfect for the role. We assign them and give them access to our lives only to discover they are the wrong fit. When you rewind the tape of your life, you will likely see the Father trying to tell you and even show you it, or they do not fit. Nevertheless, we subconsciously or even consciously

determine the Father is wrong. After this erroneous determination is made, we go on continually attempting to force
our desires to work. The harsh but true reality is that if it is
not meant for you, no amount of force will make it work. You
must trust the Father to put the pieces together and witness
the puzzle of life come together more easily.

Talk to Me God

Who or what came to mind as you read this devotional?

**Pray and give it over to God, and trust that God's will is great-
er than your will.**

Who Do You Look Like?

Therefore be imitators of God, as beloved children.

—Ephesians 5:1 (ESV)

Let this mind be in you, which was also in Christ Jesus.

—Philippians 2:5 (KJV)

One day, my son looked at me and said, "Daddy, you need to shave your beard off." I retorted, "Timothy, I like my beard. Why should I shave my beard off?" He said, "If you shave your beard, then you will look just like me." Obviously, I was flattered that my son had embraced the fact that we looked a lot alike. However, it was interesting that my son desired me to look like him rather than him looking like me. He wanted his father to adjust to his desire at the moment rather than looking forward to growing up to look like his father.

This is a depiction of us as God's children. If we are honest, there are times when we wish God would adjust to our desires in the moment rather than us adjusting to God. In reality, we desire God to look like us rather than us growing up to the degree that we look like God. Ultimately, it is our responsibility to grow up to embody the character of Christ. This entails growing up to resemble Christ in our attitude, demeanor, and actions.

<u>Talk to Me God</u>

What areas do you need to grow in to look more like Jesus?

What are some practical things you will do to grow in these areas?

189

God is Coming Through

[8] *"For my thoughts are not your thoughts, neither are your ways my ways," declares the Lord.* [9] *"As the heavens are higher than the earth, so are my ways higher than your ways and my thoughts than your thoughts.*

—Isaiah 55:8-9 (NIV)

The church I pastor was birthed on November 8, 2015. In 2023, we would celebrate our 8th birthday on Wednesday, November 8, 2023, the night we normally have Bible study. The members and I were so excited that we planned a birthday party of sorts to have as the precedent to our annual celebration the following. To my dismay, I tested positive for COVID-19 on Tuesday, November 7!!! We elected to cancel the birthday party and look toward the culmination on Sunday. While I isolated at home, church members and I prayed that I would be negative by Sunday. I tested again on the preceding Friday, and I remained positive. My heart was filled with disappointment, and I began to make calls and institute plans for a worship service that did not include me because I was positive for COVID-19. While making calls, I was convicted by the fact that I was prematurely making plans Friday for God not to come through by Sunday. My actions suggested that God could not or would not move by Sunday just because He did not move on Friday.

So often, our trust in God wavers when our prayers are not answered within a certain time. When God is not moving as we think He should, we sometimes begin to make alternate plans as if God will not come through. Whatever you are waiting to come to fruition, do not get sidetracked because things are not happening as you *think* they should. Just because it has not happened to date does not mean that it cannot happen or will not happen. It is not enough for us to say we believe God can do what we pray for; we need to act as if He can. When we pray about a need or problem, we should live and act as though we believe God can do what He says. It is better to trust God's timing and things fall into place than to move prematurely, and things fall apart. God's timing is seldom congruent with ours, but His timing is always perfect and always worth the wait.

Talk to Me God

Have you ever made alternate plans because you doubted God's timing? How did that situation turn out, and what did you learn from it?

In what areas of your life can you practice greater patience and trust in God's timing, rather than rushing ahead with your own plans?

You Still Have Value

²⁶ Brothers and sisters, think of what you were when you were called. Not many of you were wise by human standards; not many were influential; not many were of noble birth. ²⁷ But God chose the foolish things of the world to shame the wise; God chose the weak things of the world to shame the strong. ²⁸ God chose the lowly things of this world and the despised things— and the things that are not—to nullify the things that are, ²⁹ so that no one may boast before him.

Home Improvement stores like Home Depot and Lowe's have a section for appliances called the *scratch and dent* section. This is the section for appliances that have sustained some level of damage. Upper management often decides that though the appliances are damaged, they are still not so damaged that they cannot be used. The damaged appliances are discounted and purchased by people like me who do not mind a scratch or a dent but understand that that the appliance can still be used and has value despite the scratch or dent.

Ideally, life would solely comprise sunshine and rainbows, mountains exempt from the valley, all good times, all times of faring well, and never welfare. However, that is not the case. Life consists of sections in which we sustain damage. That damage can be mental, emotional, social, physical, or even spiritual. Even as you read this devotional, chances are that you have sustained damage along life's journey. Certain damage can cause you to feel that the things you have done or have been through have scratched and damaged you to the degree you have deemed yourself ineligible for whatever God has for you. You need to know that God not only can still use you, but God desires to do the extraordinary in your life. God has a tremendous habit of using imperfect people to accomplish His perfect plan. Often, the very things you think have disqualified you are the very things God wants to use. God has not disqualified you; therefore, do not disqualify yourself. God is looking for people like you and me who have incurred some scratches and dents because even with them, God has made a divine determination that you still have value.

Talk to Me God

What past experiences or imperfections make you feel disqualified from God's plans?

How has God shown you your value during times you felt broken or damaged?

God Is with You

So do not fear, for I am with you; do not be dismayed, for I am your God. I will strengthen you and help you; I will uphold you with my righteous right hand.

—Isaiah 41:10 (NIV)

[9] Have I not commanded you? Be strong and courageous. Do not be afraid; do not be discouraged, for the Lord your God will be with you wherever you go."

—Joshua 1:9 (NIV)

One day, I was teaching my son how to ride a bike so he could learn to ride the bike without assistance. I would occasionally take my hands off him and let him go on his own. When I took my hands off him, he would immediately get nervous and panicked. Removing my hands suggested that I was no longer there, and he was subject to fall. He did not realize that when I removed my hands, I jogged alongside him to make sure I could catch him in the event he needed me. However, he felt that if he could not feel me, I was not there. As his father, who loves him dearly, I had to assure him that just because he could not feel my hands did not mean my hands were not there.

Frankly, there are moments in life when it seems as if God has taken His hands off us, and we are rolling along alone (pun intended). Feeling alone can cause one to feel nervous and even panic. You can pray, and it seems your prayers seem to bounce off the ceiling. You can feel as if you are literally alone with no accompaniment. Nevertheless, the absence of feeling God does not suggest the absence of God. There are periods in life when we have to trust God when we cannot trace God. Even when you do not feel God, God is still right there. Though we are nervous and maybe even fearful, God wants us to know that He is still right there. C.S. Lewis once said, "Relying on God has to begin all over again every day as if nothing had yet been done. The great thing to remember is that though our feelings come and go, God's love for us does not." God is right there with you!

Talk to Me God

When have you felt like God was not with you, and how did you manage those feelings of loneliness and fear?

How can you remind yourself daily of God's constant presence, especially during challenging times?

Don't Let Them Burst Your Bubble

All hard work brings a profit, but mere talk leads only to poverty.

—*Proverbs 14:23 (NIV)*

A hard worker has plenty of food, but a person who chases fantasies ends up in poverty.

—*Proverbs 28:19 (NLT)*

One year, our entire family traveled to Disney World to celebrate Christmas. As we walked throughout the park, we noticed a lot of people purchasing devices that produced bubbles. Because we did not have a toy of our own, my kids and I would pop the bubbles that came in our direction that others produced. Frankly, I had both the capacity and opportunity to purchase the device and obtain the same machine. However, I did not want to pay the price to get what they possessed. We spent our time bursting into what others produced because I was unwilling to pay the price. Amazingly, the machine produced so many bubbles that some remained untouched despite our greatest effort to burst them all.

It has been said to *work as if everything depends on you, but pray as if everything depends on God.* Amazing advice to live by! However, the truth is that many people are willing to pray but are unwilling to work. Some are simply unwilling to do what is necessary to obtain the things they speak of. Unfortunately, when you achieve a measure of success in some field of human endeavor, you may find that these same people will attempt to burst your bubbles of success with negativity and other acts of jealousy whenever the opportunity presents itself. What is interesting about this is that those same people were presented with the same opportunities, yet they were unwilling to do what you did in order to get where you are. In a real sense, they can be where you are and have what you have; the sole reason they do not is simply because they were unwilling to pay the price to obtain it. Though it may be frustrating and hurtful to experience this, you can be encouraged by the fact that they can never burst out all that is within you despite their greatest effort.

Talk to Me God

How can you stay focused on your goals and maintain your motivation despite the negativity or jealousy of others?

Reflect on a time when you achieved something through hard work. How did it feel, and how can that experience inspire you to keep pushing forward?

Author Bio

Pastor Timothy Jackson, Jr. is the proud husband of Ashiqua Jackson, father of three beautiful children, Ava MaeRee, and twins, Timothy III and Avery Juliette. He serves as the Senior Pastor of Hope Fellowship Church in Memphis, Tennessee.

Pastor Jackson is a 1995 graduate of Whitehaven High School. He went on to attend the University of Tennessee at Chattanooga, where he earned a Bachelor of Science in Environmental Science with an emphasis in Biology and became a proud member of Kappa Alpha Psi Fraternity. For the fraternity, he served as Kappa League Chairman and later served as President of the chapter.

Pastor Jackson culminated his undergraduate college career by being voted the first and only African-American Mr. University of Tennessee at Chattanooga. In 2012, he graduated with a Master of Christian Studies degree from Union University. Three weeks after his graduation, he entered the Doctor of Ministry program at United Theological Seminary in Dayton, Ohio and graduated May 2015.

Jackson accepted his call to ministry September 4, 2000. Over the years, he has appeared on television, magazines, and radio along with opportunities to speak at many churches and conferences. In the early 2000s, Pastor Jackson authored an online devotional ministry entitled "Talk to Me God" that blessed the lives of thousands of people around the globe, including Australia, France and Hong Kong. Entries from the devotional ministry were published in Malaysia and the United Kingdom. Considered to be gifted with the ability to craft sermon illustrations, pastors from around the country seek him for sermon illustrations and advice in producing them. Several sermon illustrations have been published on the website of *The African American Lectionary*, providing opportunity for ministers and pastors throughout the world to tap into his gift. In addition to ministry, Pastor Jackson works as a Senior Environmental Specialist at FedEx Express Corporation, where he serves as a liaison between FedEx and environmental agencies, training employees and monitoring environmental compliance for more than 100 FedEx Express facilities throughout the United States.

Because of his wide range of pastoral and corporate experiences, he has been sought after to provide leadership advice in both corporate and church arenas. He is particularly passionate about new leaders, young ministers, and new pastors. Pastor Jackson equips them with knowledge when entering a new leadership role, and helps them avoid many of the pitfalls encountered by new leaders.

Dr. Timothy Jackson Jr.

Pastor Jackson is committed to playing an instrumental role in the building of people so that they may build up their families, communities, organizations, and churches. He strives to promote excellence spiritually, socially, and academically to people of all ages. It is his prayer that God will use him to impact the lives of people in the church, city, and nation.

Notes

Notes

Notes

Notes

Notes

Notes

Notes

Notes

Notes

Notes

Search for:

Talk To Me God Devotionals Vol. 1
by Dr. Timothy Jackson Jr.

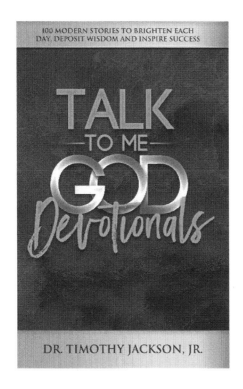

Made in the USA
Columbia, SC
06 November 2024

45813250R00124